Wisdom From Each Season

A Devotional for Married Couples

D1564003

Denise J. Ward

from various sources. Please consult a licensed professional before attempting any techniques outlined in this book.

By reading this document, the reader agrees that under no circumstances is the author responsible for any losses, direct or indirect, that are incurred as a result of the use of the information contained within this document, including, but not limited to, errors, omissions, or inaccuracies.

Table of Contents

Introduction

Many great love stories have been written and witnessed over the ages. Everyone of them contains challenges–ups and downs bestowed by the seasons encountered. The greatest of these love stories, without a doubt, echoes from the cross. The Amplified version reads in John 15:13, "No one has greater love [nor stronger commitment] than to lay down his own life for his friends." Jesus proved His love for us by laying down His life for us to ensure our place in His heavenly Kingdom.

Bruce Marchiano, the actor who portrayed Jesus in the *Matthew* film, wrote one of the most beautiful sentences ever recorded in the history of our world. In his book, *In the Footsteps of Jesus* (2000), he penned: "Jesus wasn't dragged to the cross; He was crawling to the cross— His body failing Him, struggling against all odds, a champion pushing through indescribable pain and opposition to see the fulfillment of his mission."

What makes it so much more unfathomable for the mind to comprehend is the fact that our Hero's love in this great romance is unconditional. Regardless of how sinful, petty, self-absorbed, and obstinate the recipient of this unimaginable gift is. Regardless of what the self-seeking, finger-snapping, selfish recipient of this undeserved offering does.

This is the extent of Jesus' love for us. No price is too big to pay for His bride. He sacrificed Himself for us so that we don't have to pay for our sin—a penalty we rightfully deserve.

This is the example we were given when it comes to loving an imperfect spouse, and Jesus provided the example by modeling it for us Himself.

> "Husbands, love your wives, just as Christ loved the church and gave Himself up for her to make her holy, cleansing her by the washing with water through the word, and to present her to himself as a radiant church, without stain or wrinkle or any other blemish, but holy and blameless. In this same way, husbands ought to love their wives as their own bodies. He who loves his wife loves himself. After all, no one ever hated their own body, but they feed and care for their body, just as Christ does the church—for we are members of his body. For this reason a man will leave his father and mother and be united to his wife, and the two will become one flesh.' This is a profound mystery—but I am talking about Christ and the church. However, each one of you also must love his wife as he loves himself, and the wife must respect her husband" (Ephesians 5:22-33 NIV).

I know that this verse is clearly aimed at husbands. However, I just want to focus on the example of love set for all of us. Sacrificial love. *Putting-the-needs-of-someone-else-before-my-needs* love. *Dying-unto-the-self* love.

I have read C.S. Lewis' "The Chronicles of Narnia," and usually I prefer the book to the movie, but there is something about watching Aslan's despair after he made the deal with the evil queen, Jardis, when he is delivering himself to the White Witch, when she kills him, and when he is resurrected that resonates so deeply with my spirit. Edward had been in a weak and selfish season. His betrayal of his siblings have dire consequences. Yet love remained. Love fought. Love won.

Marriage is a lot of things.

It is hard.

It is beautiful.

It is terrifying.

It is satisfying.

These aspects are part of the seasons that we find within a marriage.

If we can anchor ourselves in the powerful example that Jesus set for us, then these seasons will not be able to overtake us.

> "I can do all things [which He has called me to do] through Him who strengthens and empowers me [to fulfill His purpose—I am self-sufficient in Christ's sufficiency; I am ready for anything and equal to anything through Him who infuses me with inner strength and confident peace]" (Philippians 4:13 AMP).

Seasons change. It's a fact of life. There's consistency in the inconsistency. Consider the fact that it is possible for it to be "the coldest summer in four years," or "the winter was unseasonably warm." We find that there are things that don't pan out the way they are supposed to. Our plans are thrown out the window, altering what we were hoping for.

The trinity is the best example that we have when it comes to unity. There is no jealousy or competition. Jesus is the best example we have when it comes to unconditional, sacrificial love. He laid his life down to show the world what it truly means to love and put others first.

How This Devotional Works

This devotional can be read front-to-back, like traditional devotionals. However, because it has not been dated, it can also be read in no particular order, where you search the topics to find the one you need for that particular day. Whatever your spirit needs.

Each day's devotional ends with a prayer, reflections on the topic, and an application section. The reflections have been included as a rhetoric device, there to help you meditate on what you have learned. The application section is there for a very important reason. It is your homework, so to speak, where you have the opportunity to put into practice what you have studied that day, and incorporate the necessary change into your lifestyle to enforce the commitment you have to each other and your marriage.

Chapter 1:

Spring

No matter how long the winter, spring is sure to follow.

—African Proverb

Spring Day 1: The Snow is Melting

"For I know the plans I have for you," declares the Lord, "plans to prosper you and not to harm you, plans to give you hope and a future."

Jeremiah 29:11 (NIV)

The Deception of Perception

When we think of spring, the obvious, more romanticized pictures come to mind: flowering green fields, animals being born, running streams, and so forth. What we don't necessarily think about is the ugly: The sludge that is created when the snow melts; The barren, brown earth that still needs to be brought to life with the warmer weather; The carcasses of animals who perished during the long, hard winter that will now thaw and either be eaten or rot. While beauty exists in this season, there is also a lot of discomfort, pain, and ugliness.

How many of us enter the season of marriage with a preconceived picture firmly imprinted in our brain? A pretty picture of perfection.

If you have watched "Cool Runnings," you will remember the scene where Yul Brenner shows a picture to team mates, Sanca and Junior, of the house he sees himself living in one day. He ends up being mocked by them because the picture he so proudly flaunted was of Buckingham Palace. Brenner ended up looking and feeling like a fool. His expectations were completely unrealistic.

Do you have a picture in the league of Buckingham Palace when you think of your marriage or your spouse? Have you set an impossible standard in your heart and in your mind that will only lead to devastation and heart-break because nothing or no-one will be able to live up to that expectation? It is wise to take off any rose-tinted glasses and accept that reality is not what you find in movies, books, magazines, and social media.

Prayer:

Father God, forgive me if I have held on to a picture of what I expected my life to look like, instead of embracing Your plans for my life. Your plans and will for my life are always better than my own. Please make me aware of what I am doing when I subconsciously hurt my spouse when I compare them to the unrealistic image in my head.

Reflection:

I must give my spouse the grace to be who God created them to be.

Do I try to 'fix' or change my spouse in any way? Why is that?

Application:

Do some soul searching with your spouse. Have you ever held them or your marriage to an unobtainable standard? Have you ever tried to change them, so that they will better fit into the image you have in your mind of what your love life should look like? Ask each other for forgiveness, if necessary, and rejoice in the beauty and truth of who your spouse actually is.

Spring Day 2: Becoming

And we all… are being transformed.

2 Corinthians 3:18 (NIV)

The Start of Something Beautiful

What if the greatest gift that marriage gives, is not love or a life spouse. What if the greatest gift that marriage gives is who you get to become. -Toure Roberts

I recently watched a YouTube video where pastor and author, Toure Roberts, preaches a revelatory sermon at a marriage convention. His message is titled, "What you were never told," and for a large portion of the sermon he talks about the effects that marriage will have on us as individuals.

You are a critically important part of your marriage, and your marriage should be critically important to you.

We often assume that the main reasons Eve was created was because (a) Adam was lonely, and (b) Adam needed someone to help him rule over the dominion God had given him. But what if Eve wasn't created as a cure for Adam's loneliness? No where in scripture do read that Adam was lonely—it simply states that he was the only one of his kind. A part of me thinks he couldn't have been lonely since he was in perfect commune with Father God. Instead, what if Eve was created as a force to help Adam grow?

Roberts calls marriage an institution of transformation. There is no other relationship that will challenge us to grow the way a marriage does. Marriage simply demands it. This is God's way of saving us from the residual effects of sin. These effects include mistrust, trauma, fear, and anything left-over. He wants to heal our brokenness. Roberts states, (ONE | The Potter's House, 2020),

- You can't have a strong marriage, without a strong you.
- You can't have a whole marriage without a whole you.
- You can't have a healthy marriage, without a healthy you.

Your maturity is connected to your spouse's imperfections. And God will use those imperfections to shape and mold you into the person you were always meant to be. This is evident in Proverbs 27:17 (NIV), "As iron sharpens iron, so one person sharpens another." And, boy, does it hurt sometimes.

Prayer:

Thank You, Lord, that You care so much for me, my wellbeing, and my wholeness that you created a safe and loving place for my faults to be brought to the light. Help me not to resent my spouse when they are the tool You use to unearth my buried issues. Help me to recognize that it is You at work.

Reflection:

God uses your spouse to help you grow.

Do you embrace or spurn their help?

Application:

Think about some of the worst fights that you have had with your spouse and ask God to identify any inner wounds that were triggered or created during your arguments. Once you have a list, pray about them. Forgive the parties involved. Ask the Lord to make you whole and heal your wounds so that these triggers will be rendered ineffective.

Spring Day 3: Spring Cleaning

… They have closed their eyes…

Matthew 13:15 (NIV)

Open Your Eyes

In the 19th century, the interior of most residences were covered in soot after each winter. This was due to the burning of wood and coal for light and heat. When spring came around, the windows could be opened, and the big, and mostly unpleasant, annual clean commenced. The furniture and smaller household items were soaked, scrubbed, and buffed; bedding, rugs, and curtains were taken out and beaten until the women deemed them worthy to be in their homes again.

All too often in this polluted world of ours, we allow our eyes to be covered when we buy into lies, cultural norms, and traditions that clearly oppose the Word of the Lord.

It happens in our marriages as well. We allow our eyes to become blinded by the enemy. We no longer see how masterfully God created our spouse to be, or how God is using them to help us grow. We start believing the lies.

It happened to Leanne. She had married Daniel eight years earlier and they were blessed with two beautiful blond babies. The young family lived on Leanne's family farm to cut housing costs.

Leanne and the kids loved the experience. Each night, she would invite her parents for supper and she would make sure she honored them in all she did. It is the tenth commandment, after all. She was proud of herself for being such a considerate daughter, and she was sure the Lord felt the same. But did you notice how nothing was written about Daniel?

Daniel hated living on his father-in-law's property which prompted Leanne to label Daniel as ungrateful.

Leanne prayed, long and hard, that the Lord would change Daniel, open his eyes to the truth, and give him a heart of flesh, where there so clearly was a heart of stone! The marriage deteriorated quickly and just before the three year anniversary of moving to the farm, the d-word came up. Both parties were exhausted from all the fighting.

In a last-ditch effort, they attended a two-day marriage seminar. When a talk about "Contract vs Covenant" came up, Leanne found herself on what felt like the wrong end of a major wake-up call. The speaker explained that contract is there to protect you, whereas a covenant means:

- I pledge to protect you.
- I pledge to be there when you need me.
- We are on the same side.
- Your interests matter to me.
- You are no longer alone.

Leanne realized that she was the problem, not her husband. She had become blinded from the truth. She suddenly saw her self-righteousness and hypocrisy. She knew she hurt her husband badly when she refused to cleave to him, choosing her parents over him every single time there was an argument about the farm.

In humility, Leanne confessed to Daniel what God revealed and asked her husband to forgive her. She went to her parents and told them that there would have to be boundaries and that her husband would be prioritized over them.

The Word says in Psalm 133 that God commands His blessing where there is unity and this was obvious when they started looking for another place to live. God blessed them with a beautiful house on the exact street where they wanted to live. The house had been neglected and the owners didn't want a lot of money for it. It was a big miracle.

Prayer:

Lord, I apologize if I allowed soot to settle over my eyes, blinding me to my faults. It causes me not to see my spouse the way you see them because I have allowed hurt, pride, or self-righteousness to cloud my judgment. Give me the courage to change what I need to in order to be the best spouse my spouse deserves.

Reflection:

The Pharisees, the zealous religious leaders found in the New Testament, were so sure that they were right and Jesus was wrong. If they were foolish enough to believe that their thoughts and actions were superior to that of Jesus, and they walked and talked with Him regularly, I should know that I, too, may fall prey to self-righteousness and pride.

Do I regularly do self-examinations to check the condition of my heart—if it lines up with the Bible?

Application:

Sit with your spouse and have an open discussion about your views of each other, and any other important aspect relating to your marriage. Maybe you have forgotten who they really are to you and the true intentions of their heart. Explore any areas in which you feel you need to reevaluate. Ask the Lord to guide you through the process.

Spring Day 4: Migrations

Put up with each other, and forgive anyone who does you wrong, just as Christ has forgiven you. Love is more important than anything else. It is what ties everything completely together.

Collosians 3:13-14 (CEV)

I Smell Trouble

As a married couple, we should not avoid conflict the way some animals flee from the cold when they migrate. Conflict is not necessarily a bad thing. It induces growth both within yourself and your relationships. It's how you react to conflict that makes it positive or negative.

When it comes to dealing with conflict, there are a number of behaviors that you may exhibit. Some of the notable ones are to:

- fight
- freeze
- flee
- fix

Today, I want to focus on fleeing conflict. This could mean one of two behaviors is exhibited. The first is when you flee the conflict for the right reasons, like when you walk away from an argument before it escalates into something you may regret later on. It shows a level of maturity because you are not acting out of an emotional place. However, it is important to discuss walking away from conflict with your spouse beforehand. Tell them that, because you love them and want to honor them, you are going to put a guard over your mouth (see James 1:26, Psalm 34:13, and Psalm 39:1). This does not mean you don't want to sort out the situation, you simply recognize that the timing is not right for the discussion yet. It is unhealthy for your relationship to force a situation when one of you is angry. It seldom leads to a positive outcome.

A therapist I know advocates for a family to have a time-out word. Once someone says it, a five minute time-out is called. No one is allowed to refute it or carry on with the argument. Each member goes someplace peaceful, like outside for a quick walk, or maybe to a bedroom for breathing exercises. After the five minutes is up, the family meets up in a space of their choice. This mini-break helped everyone calm down, and collect their thoughts. Over coffee, and in a much more relaxed atmosphere, the situation is more likely to be sorted out because the threat is gone. Their brains can process information now since it is not in survival mode.

The second scenario is when you flee the situation because you don't want to deal with it. You actively avoid conflict and will do almost anything in your power not to engage with it. You either see conflict as negative, and you want to avoid it, or it might be that something in your past has traumatized you to the extent where you feel like you may have a meltdown or panic attack if faced with conflict. Everything in your body screams at you, and forces you to flee the situation.

You are doing your relationship a disservice if you continually flee from conflict. However, as with the first type of fleeing, as a couple, you should have a strategy on how to handle the situation.

If you see your spouse is becoming antsy, suggest reconvening in a few minutes or just use the time-out word. If it helps to assure them with physical contact, then hug your spouse. Do whatever is necessary to create an atmosphere where growth can happen.

You may think it silly, or foreign, to talk about strategies for conflict resolution, but they can be a tremendous help in your marriage.

Prayer:

Lord God, when conflict situations arise, help me to remember that I am dealing with one of your precious children, and not someone I get to use as a proxy for a verbal punching bag. Teach me how to handle conflict in a godly way.

Reflection:

Conflict does not need to be negative, but I need to be sensitive to the needs of my spouse when it comes to creating a safe space for them to deal with it.

In what areas am I insensitive to my spouse's feelings and needs?

How can I help to create a safe space for our difficult conversations or disagreements?

Application:

Have a discussion about how conflict was handled in your childhood homes and how it has shaped your views about conflict management. Next, work out a strategy for when conflict arises in your home.

Spring Day 5: New Leaves

… put off your old self, which belongs to your former manner of life and is corrupt through deceitful desires, and to be renewed in the spirit of your minds, and to put on the new self, created after the likeness of God in true righteousness and holiness.

Ephesians 4:22-24 (ESV)

Turning Over A New Leaf

I am sorry are words that are almost as mighty as *I love you.* You have probably experienced the power of a sincere apology so you know it has the ability to set you free and completely overhaul a difficult situation.

However, without a change in behavior, those short three words end up meaning nothing. Can a person be truly apologetic without mending their ways?

Even worse, if it is simply lip-service, then it is not much different from a lie.

I explain the concept as playacting. I would lightly slap someone on the arm and apologize. Then I repeat those two actions again and again, carefully watching the face of the person who is being slapped. After a while, they don't find it amusing anymore. It is the same in any other situation.

When you apologize for behavior that has wronged your spouse, you have to actively work at not doing it again. *I'm sorry* should equate to *I will not do it again.*

We make it harder and harder for the person we have wronged to forgive us and trust us when our behaviors don't change.

Turning over a new leaf, means doing a complete 180 degree turn. The front of the leaf looks different from its back since the back contains more stomata.

To change a behavior is not an easy task, but it is not impossible. Nothing is impossible, remember. I am not taking God out of the picture here. He can and will bring restoration when asked. We have the power of Christ, the love we have for our spouse, and our choice to drive change.

However, this does not give us the right to snap their fingers and demand change where change is not necessary. This type of authoritarian behavior is not consistent with Jesus' teachings.

Prayer:

Father, change is hard but necessary. Please strengthen and equip me so that I can change where I need to in order to preserve the harmony in my marriage.

Reflection:

I am not the only one in my marriage. Sometimes I need to make adjustments for my relationship to thrive.

What adjustments do I need to make in my relationship?

Application:

Make a list of your relationship priorities. Ask yourself how your behavior affects these priorities. If need be, take it a step further by drawing up a pros and cons list to examine your actions. Do they serve your relationship, or work against it?

Spring Day 6: More Exposure to Light

And this I pray, that your love may abound still more and more in real knowledge and all discernment, so that you may approve the things that are excellent, in order to be sincere and blameless until the day of Christ; having been filled with the fruit of righteousness which comes through Jesus Christ, to the glory and praise of God.

Philippians 1:9-11 (ESV)

Revelation

When spring comes, daylight hours increase. When we think of the idiomatic phrase "to shed more light" on something we realize that there are actions involved that bring more insight, revelation, and/or clarity.

The longer we are in a relationship with someone, the better we get to know them. This is somewhat of a blessing and a curse. The former because it increases intimacy and transparency; the latter because it exposes the parts of us that we would rather keep hidden.

There is so much freedom if we can be our honest and truthful selves in a relationship. Granted that the consistent atmosphere in your marriage should be one of unconditional acceptance and love.

I watched the movie *Eight Mile*, a flick loosely based on the life of rapper Eminem. While this is not a movie I would typically watch, I am grateful that I saw it. It provided me with a revelation that I value to this day.

When we are open and honest about our struggles, and confess our sins (see 1 John 1:9), then the enemy loses a foothold in our life. While I recognize that we can't always trust everyone to respond respectfully with the information we relay regarding our experiences, there is a release when we bring that which we try desperately to hide, to the forefront. More often than not, it is a futile struggle trying to keep secrets hidden, as they tend to come out eventually.

Alongside this, we should base our identity in Christ, and when we find our worth in Him, it won't matter what others think of us or say about us. Stealing a truth from another movie, *The Way Way Back,* often what others think of us says more about them than it does about us.

Prayer:

Lord, may we grow more comfortable to reveal our faults, flaws, and fails to our spouse. May our past lose its hold on us as we allow Your truth to set us free.

Reflection:

I decide what has power over me. Do I give my power away to one of my facial features—my nose, perhaps? Or am I allowing something else to dictate how I feel about myself? Am I like a thermometer that merely accepts the temperature and reflects it to the world, or am I a thermostat that regulates the temperature and changes it when necessary?

Application:

Ask the Lord to provide you with a time and place where you can speak to your spouse about the elements of the past that are keeping you prisoner. Ask them to pray with you.

Note: Sometimes it is better to first speak to a counselor, therapist, or psychologist before attempting the conversation with your loved one. If this is the case, speak to the person you feel God has brought you to, but never stop trusting God for an opportunity to eventually have this conversation with your spouse. Please note that it is much better to seek help from someone who is of the same sex as you. Intense emotions and moments can encourage doors that lead to inappropriate relationships.

Spring Day 7: A Fresh View

Jesus knew their thoughts and replied, "Any kingdom divided by civil war is doomed. A town or family splintered by feuding will fall apart."

Matthew 12:25 (NLT)

Sticking Together

Spring is synonymous with the word 'fresh.' We just have to look around during the few months where spring rules our corner of the universe to understand why. Everything looks new, clean, and well, fresh.

Another thing that is synonymous with 'fresh' is *The Fresh Prince of Bel-Air*, a hit comedy series of the 1990s which stars Will Smith.

> "According to *Zook*, *The Fresh Prince of Bel-Air* was created as an attempt to disrupt 'black-on-black prejudice' among 'haves and have-nots.' In other words, the purpose of the show was to stop the discrimination and hate between upper-class and lower-class blacks" (Bissoy, n.d.).

The way I interpret this is that there was a group of people who should have stuck together, but instead let their selfish nature, differences, and grandiose ideas of superiority come between them.

Sound familiar? Don't we do that in our marriage? For one or the other reason we discriminate against our spouse, driving a wedge between us. Then we are too blind to recognize what we are doing.

The enemy has a way of making us forget who our true opponent is. Instead, he somehow shines a spotlight on our spouse, and we fixate all our negative energy on our spouse. Then the real bad guy sits back and enjoys the show of us fighting each other instead of him.

Prayer:

Open my eyes, Lord, when I become misguided, self-absorbed, mean, and self-righteous. Remind me that we are on the same team, fighting a common adversary who will stop at nothing to separate us. Instead of criticizing, may I build-up, bless, and encourage my spouse.

Reflection:

Peace in a home is priceless. What do I do to make my home less peaceful? Do I prioritize being right, over being kind?

Application:

When you recognize that you have fallen for the enemy's ploy to make your spouse out to be the foe, stop and go on the offensive. Instead of complaining, sing a praise song to the Lord; instead of criticizing, pray for your loved one; instead of convincing, listen to your spouse; instead of judging, love them.

Spring Day 8: Warmer Weather

Hot tempers cause arguments, but patience brings peace.

Proverbs 15:18 (GNT)

When Tensions Rise

When spring comes, the temperature rises and it gets warmer.

When there is a lot going on in our work, relationships, and finances, especially when there are things that feel out of our control, tensions increase. If not given the proper attention, these tensions rise and on one unfortunate day, they erupt.

Oftentimes your spouse will be on the receiving end of your frustrations as you may not be able to voice your agitation to the person who caused the build up. Maybe it is your boss that is being unfair, a colleague who is being unreasonable, or even a random driver who puts you at risk on the road. Because your anger could not be dealt with, it simply found a spot in your body, laid down, and waited for an opportune time to be expelled. Quite accidentally your spouse said or did something and it triggered an underserved outburst from you.

You, more than your home, are supposed to be your spouse's safe place. Work hard to keep it that way, otherwise it may become a habit that leaves your spouse feeling like they are your verbal punching bag. Marriage was never meant to be like that.

Prayer:

Father, in accordance with Psalm 141:3, I want to ask You to set a guard over my mouth, Lord, and keep watch over the door of my lips. Let me not hurt my spouse, whom I love dearly, with the eruptions of anger that I mistakenly direct at them. Help me to rule over my emotions, and work through them in a positive and life-bringing manner.

Reflection:

My spouse is not my verbal punching bag.

Do I sometimes treat them as one? If that is the case, what can I do to prevent it from happening?

Application:

When you feel stressed, with the possibility of tensions rising even more, make an appointment with your spouse to discuss what is going on in your life. Be open and honest. Pray for each other and encourage each other during these difficult times. If possible, have this discussion while you are taking a walk. The little bit of exercise will help to decrease tension-levels and leave you feeling calmer. I can attest that it works as I can see what it does for my husband and me. It helps us destress, share our hearts, and establish a deeper connection with each other.

Spring Day 9: Planting a Garden

"For this reason a man will leave his father and mother and be united to his wife, and the two will become one flesh[.] So they are no longer two, but one flesh. Therefore what God has joined together, let no one separate."

Matthew 19:5-6 (BSB)

Leaving and Cleaving

Spring time is the ideal time to plant a garden and become more self-sufficient.

One of the things that I will probably never forget that a pastor told me and my husband before we got married, was that I should forget my family's potato salad recipe and my husband should forget his family's potato salad recipe. It was now up to us to create our own recipe.

This was the pastor's inelegant, but very effective, way of telling us that once we're married, it is important to (a) leave our parents' home—physically, emotionally, and mentally, and (b) find what works for us.

That pastor qualified his potato salad command by telling us that in his experience, the "irreconcilable differences" written on the divorce papers basically spells out "in-law trouble."

While asking for advice from the in-laws is a good, even biblical, concept, if they are exhibiting behavior contrary to the Word, it is necessary to ignore it. This can be hard for the spouse whose parents gave the advice. It may seem like a form of betrayal. However, it is more important to follow godly principles, especially when it comes to saving or prioritizing your marriage.

Prayer:

Lord, if I am still, in any way, cleaving to either my parents or their way of doing things, please expose it to me. Help me to fully commit and cleave to my spouse. I want my spouse to know that when I have to choose between my parents or my marriage, that my marriage will always take priority.

Reflection:

The Word is very clear about leaving my parents' home and cleaving to my spouse. It is mentioned in both the Old and the New Testament.

Is there an area in my life where I am still, figuratively, stuck in my parents' house? How is it affecting my marriage?

Application:

Have an open and honest conversation with your spouse and ask them if they perceive a hold that your parents may have on you. It may not be the easiest of conversations but "[i]f you pay attention when you are corrected, you are wise" (Proverbs 15:31 GNT).

Spring Day 10: Beauty

... clothe yourself with splendor and majesty.

Psalm 45:3b (NIV)

Dressed for Success

Self-care is the actions you do, to take care of yourself. It can be anything from eating healthy food to showering at night. Unfortunately, it is all too easy to fall in a rut of comfort when it comes to self-care in a marriage. The initial stage of trying your best to make a good impression fades over time.

And, while the external is never as important as the internal, it does not mean that we get to neglect ourselves on the outside.

Sometimes our 'look' betrays a little truth about a bad self-image—and what a pendulum swing there is to that statement! It can go from dressing badly because that is how I feel about myself, to trying to mimic Disco Barbie because I am over-compensating.

Remember that you created an expectation for them when you took great care dressing for your spouse during your courtship.

A good friend of mine asks her husband's opinion when she dresses in the morning. It has created a special bond between them as he feels valued and she feels like a million bucks knowing he finds her look attractive. This may not work for all couples, however, there are still ways in which we can consider one another.

During a previous holiday, my husband asked me not to wear a particular shirt that I had previously received quite a number of compliments for wearing. He qualified his request by saying it made me look like an old lady.

It is amazing how a comment like that can trigger a whole lot of buried issues. I was so grateful that I could feel the Holy Spirit with me, guiding me through what was happening in my heart.

I had to realize that

- My husband didn't call me ugly.
- It was my shirt that he didn't like.
- He was asking me to value his opinion.
- I have told him to change his clothes plenty of times before without considering how it might make him feel.
- This situation can bring us closer together if I handle it correctly.

I asked my husband to describe an outfit that he likes to see me in, and with my bare basic holiday wardrobe, I tried to recreate it as best as possible. I will not forget the look on that man's face. He knew I dressed especially for him. This made getting rid of the "old lady" shirt quite easy.

I have set a standard for myself when dressing in the morning. Even if I wear sweatpants, I can still look good if I do a little something-something to my hair, and maybe wear a cute pair of earrings.

This does not mean that we base our identity in our looks. It is based on what our Heavenly Father says about us and what Jesus Christ did for us. However, feeling pretty does something to a female; just look at a young girl twirling in her dress. And, knowing that your lady dressed with you in mind, does something to the heart of your man.

Prayer:

Lord, our world is driven by an idea of perfection propagated by social media, magazines, and advertising. Help us to root our identity in You. Help us, also, to consider the needs of our spouses, and without becoming their version of me, to dress in a way that they know I want to look good for them.

Reflection:

What message am I sending my spouse and the world by the way I practice self-care?

Application:

Have an open and honest conversation with your spouse about what you find attractive and what you don't. It doesn't have to be limited to clothes. Choose your words carefully; you don't want a conversation that is meant to bring you closer, to drive you apart.

Spring Day 11: Flowers

... the Lord is the maker of them all.

Proverbs 22:2 (ESV)

A Bounty of Color, Shape, and Size

A short walk in nature is evidence enough that God loves variety. Simply look at the flowers He created. There are over 400,000 varieties already cataloged with over 2,000 new flowers being discovered each year.

God included his love for diversity when He created the human race—externally and internally. Having said this, how often do we criticize our spouse for thinking, feeling, and acting differently to what we would consider correct?

There is a line in the 2004 classic, *Bride and Prejudice*, where the female protagonist, Lalita, puts Mr. Darcy in his place by saying it is wrong to impose his standards on others. I am often reminded of this line when I expect others to behave the way I would in any given circumstance.

It is not wrong to have a specific way of doing things, in fact, we all have behaviors that make sense to us. Our personalities and our upbringing play a big role here.

Different is just that—different. Not wrong. Not less than. Not, not good enough. Just different. And different is good.

Prayer:

Father, thank You for the intricate and meticulous way You created every aspect of me. Thank You for the intricate and meticulous way You created my spouse. Help us to celebrate our differences.

Reflection:

"Variety's the very spice of life, That gives it all its flavor" —William Cowper.

Do I accept my partner unconditionally, and instead of dictating their behavior, do I celebrate the different flavors that we add to the world?

Application:

Learn to identify and stop yourself when you are being unfairly biased to your spouse's behavior. Accept that God made them to think, feel, and act in a way conducive to their calling. This may vary from the way you think, feel, and act. For example, if your spouse is a realist, designed by the Lord to predict, investigate, and solve problems, don't criticize them for not being an optimist like you.

Spring Day 12: Increased Energy

But those who hope in the Lord will renew their strength. They will soar on wings like eagles; they will run and not grow weary, they will walk and not be faint.

Isaiah 40:31 (NIV)

Plug Into God

Due to an increase in sunlight in the spring, the fauna and flora are able to source more energy from their surroundings. In a similar way, we are able to extract energy and strength from our Heaven Father as He is an endless supply of power to us.

When we are weak, we simply have to turn to Him and plug into Him to obtain the energy we need to carry on. It says in the Word in 2 Corinthians 12:9-11 NKJV,

> "But He said to me, 'My grace is sufficient for you, for My power is made perfect in weakness.' Therefore I will boast all the more gladly about my weaknesses, so that Christ's power may rest on me. That is why, for Christ's sake, I delight in weaknesses, in insults, in hardships, in persecutions, in difficulties. For when I am weak, then I am strong."

There is another section in the Old Testament that brings great encouragement, "The Sovereign Lord is my strength; he makes my feet like the feet of a deer, he enables me to tread on the heights," (Habakkuk 3:19 NIV).

> "The deer, or hind, referenced here can also be called a gazelle, a graceful, swift, and sure-footed animal that can climb sheer rocky cliffs and never stumble or fall. In climbing, the deer can place her back feet exactly where her front feet were, thus needing only two sturdy footrests instead of four. She can scamper across what appears to be a vertical cliff, unafraid and undeterred by seemingly impassable terrain" (Got Questions Ministries, 2022).

Regardless of the marital circumstances we find ourselves in, whether *seemingly impassable*, excruciatingly tough, terrifying, mundane, or heartbreaking, God has what we need to carry on. Marriages are important to Him because their reach is far and wide and very consequential.

Prayer:

Teach me, Lord, to always turn to You first during times of trouble. Help me to source my strength from You and to be unafraid of the situations I face. May I remember that my problems, every issue I face, has an expiration date.

Reflection:

Since God is a God of relationship, He can and will provide you with what you need during any season of marital difficulty. Do you trust Him to do this?

Application:

The next time you reach for your phone during times of hardship, whether it is to phone a friend, text a loved one, or google something, stop yourself. Find a quiet spot and empty your heart out to the Lord. Meditate on the promises found in the Word. Speak them out loud.

Spring Day 13: Allium

A person standing alone can be attacked and defeated, but two can stand back-to-back and conquer. Three are even better, for a triple-braided cord is not easily broken.

Ecclesiastes 4:12 (NLB)

Unity: A Superpower

The allium flower symbolizes "good fortune and prosperity, but also unity, patience, humility, and grace… The symbolism of unity comes from the fact that the flowers are clustered into a single spherical bloom and develop from a single bulb," (Forbes, 2022).

Unity does not mean you and your spouse need to be mirror copies of each other with the same opinions, taste, and aspirations. That would be immensely boring. I wouldn't want to be married to myself.

Drawing from what Maddie Forbes wrote about the flower developing from a single bulb, we can infer it means having the same foundation. I often describe it as doing life with the same rules.

In an online article pertaining to unity, Mark Merrill (2017) states that, "Unity between a husband and wife is the anchor that steadies a couple in the storms and the fuel that sustains them for the long haul." It is so important and precious to Father God that He commands His blessing there where He finds unity.

"Behold, how good and how pleasant it is for brethren to dwell together in unity! It is like the precious ointment upon the head, that ran down upon the beard, even Aaron's beard: that went down to the skirts of his garments; As the dew of Hermon, and as the dew that descended upon the mountains of Zion: for there the Lord commanded the blessing, even life forevermore" (Psalm 133 KJV).

It can honestly be regarded as a superpower in marriage. "Again, I tell you truly that if two of you on the earth agree about anything you ask for, it will be done for you by My Father in heaven. For where two or three gather together in My name, there am I with them" (Matthew 18:19-20 BSB).

Prayer:

Father God, because unity is so important in a marriage, I ask that you will give me a special anointing to both pursue it and recognize when my thoughts, attitudes, words, and actions are in opposition to it. Help us as a couple to fully comprehend what unity is and how it can bless our marriage.

Reflection:

Unity is a vital ingredient for a successful marriage. What can you do to promote unity in your marriage?

Application:

Everytime Fleetwood Mac gets stuck in your head and you want to *Go Your Own Way*, measure the consequences of unity (commanded blessing, the presence of the Lord, answered prayer) against the consequences of disunity.

Note: Your allegiance is first and foremost to God. If your spouse expects things from you that goes against the will of the Father, then your priority should always be pleasing Him.

Spring Day 14: The Purple Hyacinth

My soul is weary with sorrow; strengthen me according to your word.

Psalm 119:28 (NIV)

Sorrow

Back in the day when lovers still communicated in the language of flowers, the purple hyacinth is a flower no one really wanted. It represents sorrow and as we all can attest to, sorrow comes from dark places.

Many relationships crack and eventually fall apart during times of severe stress, trauma, or loss. The despair feels too overwhelming and strong—a battle too hard to continue fighting.

I had a conversation with God once about how cruel and unfair death is. While He didn't reply with words, He did lead me to a burnt field on a farm. He showed me how the smoldering black patch of devastation can be transformed into the most luxuriant plot of green.

God did the same with Job. Out of the wreckage that was left of the broken man's life, God brought a double portion of blessing. This economy is often difficult for us to comprehend.

Romans 8:28, in the New Living Translation, says, "And we know that God causes everything to work together for the good of those who love God and are called according to his purpose for them."

The key is to be each other's safe space during the storm. Remember the quote, "Storms make trees take deeper roots."

Prayer:

Jesus, it brings me comfort to know that You are well acquainted with sorrow. You were betrayed by those closest to You, rejected by those who claimed to know Your Father, tortured by those very people You came to save. Your time on earth was not easy. May I follow in Your example never to allow sorrow to overtake and cripple me. May I hold on to You, the way You held on to the Father during times of grief. Help my spouse and I to hold on to each other as well and not allow circumstances to break us apart.

Reflection:

Sorrow need not be a dividing factor. It could bring you and your spouse closer together.

Has there been any tragedy from the past that has come between you? What exactly caused the rift and how can it be overcome?

Application:

If and when sorrow shows up in your relationship, work together to create a safe space for you to work through it together. Give each other grace to deal with the situation however necessary. Don't forget to invite

God into the situation and to rely on His wisdom and strength to pull you through.

Chapter 2:

Summer

One must maintain a little bit of summer even in the middle of winter.

—Henry David Thoreau

Summer Day 1: Hello Heat!

... and they shall become one flesh.

Genesis 2:24 (NASB)

The Precious Gift of Sex

In summer, the heat is one of the most prevalent elements that is welcomed and celebrated.

We celebrate heat in a marriage as well. Sex is one of the most important aspects of a marriage. It is just a pity that it is so undervalued, misunderstood, and misused.

The desire for physical intimacy with your spouse is healthy and normal. It is a craving created by the Lord and should not be seen as sinful. Desire is the starting point of a sexual encounter with your spouse. Don't be embarrassed by it. There is nothing wrong with it.

Like with so many other things God has created, the enemy has perverted the act of love-making as an attempt to disrupt a couple's sex life. These upsets can cause huge rifts in a marriage as sex is a foundatinal component. Unfortunately, so many Christians buy into this false representation of this experience that God created to unify, pleasure, and fulfill His children.

Men usually need sex more than women do. "The typical wife doesn't understand her husband's deep need for sex any more than the typical husband understands his wife's deep need for affection" (Harley, 2020). If a husband can master meeting his wife's craving for affection and emotional connection, his wife is more likely to engage in the physical pleasure that he craves.

Prayer:

Lord God, thank You for sex. Rectify my views about it if my upbringing, past experiences, or the enemy have distorted it. I want to enjoy the act of love-making with my spouse, both in the giving and receiving aspects.

Reflection:

Sex, performed in the sanctity of marriage, is godly, beautiful, fulfilling, and necessary. How do you see sex? What leads you to form your opinion about it? Do your beliefs line up with the Word?

Application:

As uncomfortable and foreign as it may seem, have a conversation with your spouse about sex. Discuss every element that you need to, from the viewpoint that you were raised with, to your fears, needs, and expectations. Talk about what you are comfortable with, and what you are not willing to entertain.

Unless told otherwise by Father God, hold off talking to each other about past experiences that don't involve your spouse. This is a conversation that may do more harm than good. But since it is biblical to confess all sin (see Proverbs 28:13, James 5:16, and I John 1:9), seek out the right person who will listen to you and pray with you to loosen any hold that your sexual past may have on you and your offspring.

Forgive your spouse for any previous sexual encounters and do not hold it against your spouse.

Summer Day 2: Sunshine and Sunflowers

Let us fix our eyes on Jesus, the author and perfecter of our faith, who for the joy set before him endured the cross, scorning its shame, and sat down at the right hand of the throne of God. Consider him who endured such opposition from sinful men, so that you will not grow weary and lose heart.

Hebrews 12:2-4 (NIV)

Keeping Our Eyes on Jesus

Summer is a beautiful season marked with growth, life, and the buzz of activity. It also has a special radiance to it when the rays of sunshine dance through the branches of trees and other tall-growing plants.

There is a majestic beauty when walking through a field of sunflowers in the late afternoon. We know that these flowers track the movement of the sun to attract bees, reproduce more successfully, and absorb as much energy as they can.

What a lesson that God is trying to teach us through the nature of a sunflower!

We should also always look to Jesus. It is only by studying Him that we can be truly effective in our Christian walk.

In Exodus 34 we read how Moses' face becomes radiant after spending time with Father God on Mount Sinai. This means that it becomes evident when we have made an effort to spend time with the Lord. We reflect His glory.

Prayer:

God, You are incredible. I can see this when I look at Your creation. You so intricately planned everything out in the greatest detail. You added so much significance to Your designs. Thank You for what I can learn by studying You and Your world. May this time I spend in Your presence also be beneficial to my spouse as I try to reflect Your image to them.

Reflection:

May the radiance of Jesus always be visible when those around you interact with you.

If you can't see that you are reflecting Jesus as the light of the world and the salt of the earth, ask yourself why that is so.

Application:

Stop yourself from being on your tech devices too frequently. They are really not good for your mental wellbeing—physically or emotionally. They cause you to lose focus and concentrate less as your mind engages in mindless activities for far too long. Instead, have regular set times where you seek the Lord, read His Word, meditate on scriptures, and praise Him. Learning how to be more like Jesus is much better for your future.

Summer Day 3: A Hidden Beach

As they traveled along, Jesus entered a village where a woman named Martha welcomed Him into her home. She had a sister named Mary, who sat at the Lord's feet listening to His message. But Martha was distracted by all the preparations to be made. She came to Jesus and said, "Lord, do You not care that my sister has left me to serve alone? Tell her to help me!"

"Martha, Martha," the Lord replied, "you are worried and upset about many things. But only one thing is necessary. Mary has chosen the good portion, and it will not be taken away from her."

Luke 10:38-42 (BSB)

Less of the World, More of You

There are few things as pleasant as being the only people on a secluded beach. Apart from having the freedom to do what you want, you have a life-giving space that doesn't drain you emotionally or mentally. It's a cleaner, safer, more spacious place where we can relax and be revived.

Our relationship with our spouse is like a hidden beach. Reconnecting with our spouse yields a variety of benefits for the relationship. But it also does a lot for us as individuals.

In the Bible we have Mary and Martha as examples. Mary didn't feel the need to perform when she was in Jesus' presence. She could simply just be. I think those times helped her to grow, heal, and establish her identity.

Martha chose performance over presence. It hurt her relationship with Jesus. She was fixating on the negative, criticizing her loved ones and reaching burn-out.

When I get busy running our business and my plate is full with duties and responsibilities, I have to intentionally make time for my husband. Special time with him fills my tank, refreshes my mind, and restores my peace. It gives me what I need to be successful in my daily activities.

Prayer:

Thank You, God, that You never leave my side and that you provide me with the courage and strength I need to face any buried issues I have. Thank You for giving me a spouse that will face my storms with me.

Reflection:

Spending time in God's presence is a necessity for a healthy, peaceful, joyful and productive life. The same can be said of spending time basking in the love of your spouse. We are created as relational beings. Relationships matter.

Do you create a restorative atmosphere when you are around your partner?

Application:

Try to spend at least 10 minutes a day alone with your spouse. Focus on making the atmosphere as loving and safe as possible. Be very careful with what you discuss. It should be an affirming time for both marriage partners.

Phone each other regularly. Boost your spouse. Let them know they are a priority.

Summer Day 4: Sunscreen

Get all the advice and instruction you can, so you will be wise the rest of your life.

Proverbs 19:20 (NLT)

"Advice, like youth, probably just wasted on the young"

A very famous essay was written by columnist Mary Schmich and published in the Chicago Tribune in 1997. It made such an impact on readers (both the content and the fact that it was miscredited to Kurt Vonnegut) that director Baz Luhrmann took the essay in its entirety and put it to music. This created the chart-topping hit that is commonly referred to as the sunscreen song.

The essay-turned-song, *Everybody's Free*, is formatted as a commencement speech and humorously dispenses advice after the opening line, "Ladies and Gentlemen of the Class of '97."

I can't help but wonder how many people actually followed the advice given. It is so much easier to be the one endowing the wisdom, than the one on the receiving end who then has to make the difficult decision of whether or not to follow the advice.

Do you have mentors or spiritual advisors in place to help you when things get hard in your marriage? Or do you prefer the lone ranger route, perfectly happy to handle everything on your own? In Proverbs 15:22 (NIV) we read, "Plans fail for lack of counsel, but with many advisers they succeed."

We know that following a recipe, with care and precision, will produce the best results. Recipes have been tried and tested by experts and scientists. We know that we can follow their advice, and their counsel when things go wrong in the kitchen. In my life, as the youngest of three children, I had the advantage of learning from the blunders that my siblings made. They tried and tested quite a few things. Drawing from their wisdom and experience allowed me not to make the costly, even disastrous, mistakes they did.

Prayer:

Father, help me to receive advice graciously from those that have proven themselves to be godly and wise. Allow me to recognize my shortcomings and not be too proud to ask for help.

Reflection:

Learning from the mistakes made by others is much easier than learning from having made those mistakes myself.

What is it that causes me to make mistakes in the first place? Are some of them deliberate?

Application:

When you go through difficult times, ask yourself if there is anyone in your life that you trust and respect, who can provide you with the necessary input and wisdom you need to triumph over circumstances. Pray about it, and if you and your spouse feel the Spirit leading you, make an appointment with that person to seek their guidance.

Summer Day 5: Holiday Heaven

"… Arise, come, my darling; my beautiful one, come with me."

Song of Solomon 2:13b

Romantic Getaways

While date nights are vital for a healthy relationship, they are simply not enough to sustain a marriage. Taking a break from work and other daily responsibilities, and giving ourselves completely to our spouse for extended periods of time can yield very powerful results. It strengthens our relationship while sending a very clear message to our spouse telling them how important they are to us.

Other benefits of a romantic getaway may include:

- giving us something to look forward to
- showing our spouse how much we care by planning something special for them
- making epic memories
- giving our our full attention and enjoy how they blossom under all the personal care
- allowing us to decrease our stress levels by focussing on something other than work and worries
- improving mental health and creativity
- rekindling the romance

- improving intimacy

Know that it isn't the amount of money spent on a getaway that matters. It is the amount of effort that goes into it. It is the small things that make the difference.

Prayer:

Father God, as I make going away with my spouse a priority, please provide what is necessary to make the time together as precious as possible. Help me connect with my marriage in ways that will fill their love tank and help them to realize how grateful I am to be married to them.

Reflection:

"Getting away together can breathe new life into your marriage. Making it happen isn't always easy. But it's always worth it," —Selah Home.

What is stopping me from taking a trip with my spouse? Is there anything I can do to facilitate a trip?

Application:

Plan a romantic trip for your spouse where your aim is to bless them, love them, nourish them, and build them up.

Summer Day 6: Overcrowding

"Enter through the narrow gate. For wide is the gate and broad is the road that leads to destruction, and many enter through it. But small is the gate and narrow the road that leads to life, and only a few find it."

Matthew 7:13-14 (NIV)

Walking the Straight and Narrow

When summer comes along, there are several popular destinations that draw people like magnets. Unfortunately, some of the reasons why these spots are crowd pleasers are less than stellar: there's an abundance of drinking, gambling, promiscuity, drugs, et cetera. This translates into a whole bunch of other issues as well, ranging from littering to fighting to problems with infrastructure. Yet people keep going to these places. Gratifying the lusts of the flesh has quite the appeal, until someone gets hurt. And they all too often do.

It is especially challenging if those around you tend to favor the big, broad way and expect you to do the same.

Some people have criticized marriage as being confining, boring, and hard. And let's be honest—it can be. Sticking to the narrow road doesn't necessarily illicit visions of joy, fun, and pleasure. While it is never going to be perfect, a godly marriage can be an enjoyable, healthy, life-giving, safe space. There are a myriad of benefits in playing by the rules when it comes to marriage.

It offers, among other things,

- spiritual, emotional, and physical intimacy
- companionship
- unconditional love and acceptance
- support
- commitment
- personal growth

Prayer:

Lord, thank You that You have my best interests at heart even when it seems like You don't want me to have fun. Remind me of the detriments of following conventional wisdom and the benefits of staying on the narrow path.

Reflection:

"But you are a chosen race, a royal priesthood, a holy nation, a people for His own possession, that you may proclaim the excellencies of Him who called you out of darkness into His marvelous light," 1 Peter 2:9 (ESV).

"But know that the Lord has set apart the godly for Himself; the Lord hears when I call to Him," Psalm 4:3 (ESV).

Do these verses reflect in my life and marriage? Do people see that I have been called out of darkness and set apart to be holy, as God is holy?

Application:

Show the world that you have been set apart and called to a higher standard of living. Do this especially when dealing with your spouse. Treat them with the love and respect that Christ has for His body.

Summer Day 7: Showing a Little More Skin

This is how love is made complete among us so that we will have confidence on the day of judgment: In this world we are like Jesus.

I John 4:17 (NIV)

Being Confident Enough to Reveal More of Yourself

Summer means less clothes. The higher temperatures and the swimming pool demands it. Less clothes, however, means that more confidence is needed.

Having someone who loves us unconditionally instills a confidence in us that allows us to walk with our head held a little higher. We tap into their opinion of us— someone sees us and deems us worthy enough of their love, time, and attention—and our worth increases. It helps us to care less about the opinions of others because our self-image has improved. Alongside this, we feel freer to reveal our true selves so we break down the walls we built up for protection.

It is important to be a source of confidence for our spouse. They need to know that we see them, value them, protect them, love them, and cherish them. We also need to remind them of God's opinion of them. He is their true source of confidence.

Prayer:

Lord, may my spouse and I never forget that our worth
is based in You, and You thought we are worth dying
for. Help us to grow in Your love and be anchored in
Your thoughts of us. May we step into the light,
unafraid of the opinions of others, and be the salt that
this world needs.

Reflection:

Søren Kierkegaard: "Now, with God's help, I shall
become myself."

Do I accept God's opinion of myself, or am I still
constantly trying to prove myself? Conversely, am I the
type of spouse who builds my partner's confidence?

Application:

When there are times that you want to withdraw and
hide from others, whether it is in a conversation or
uncomfortable situation, remind yourself that you are a
cherished child of the King of the universe. Draw
strength and courage from the love of your heavenly
Father and your spouse and force yourself to step out
into the light. When you see your spouse falter in this
area, reaffirm their identity in Christ. Encourage them
to accept, love, and value themselves.

Summer Day 8: Strawberries

"You have captivated my heart, my sister, my bride; you have captivated my heart with one glance of your eyes, with one jewel of your necklace."

Song of Solomon 4:9 (NIV)

Date Night

Summer ripened strawberries dipped in chocolate (or caramel, if you are more like me) is such a decadent date night treat.

In his article, "Five Lesser-Known Reasons Why Date Night Is Important" Gal Szekely starts off by listing the better known reasons why it is important to make time to go out with your spouse—"it fosters communication, increases feelings of intimacy, decreases the chances of taking each other for granted, decreases stress, and builds attachment" (Szekely, 2017).

He then lists another five reasons why investing in regular date nights could mean for your marriage.

1. Joy will feature more prominently in your life since you know you are important to someone and they are taking the time and effort to spend special moments with you.

2. As you are investing in your marriage, you are drastically decreasing your chances of getting a divorce.
3. More dates usually translates into more sex.
4. The special attention and care bestowed on the wives increase their overall satisfaction in marriage up to seven times.
5. When the parents are happier, the children tend to be happier.

Everyone desires attention from their spouse. And the sad thing is that if the spouse is not there to bestow the attention, there usually is someone else who is more than willing to step up and fill the void.

Prayer:

Lord God, during these rushed and hectic times that we live it is so easy to deprioritize date night. And because our partner knows that we have so much on our plate, they all too easily accept being placed on a back burner. Help me to reevaluate my priorities and to make time for the most important person in my life. I don't want to lose my spouse, especially not if it is in my power to keep them by my side.

Reflection:

The benefits of spending quality time with your beloved are astronomical. Do you go out of your way to spend time with your husband, nurturing your relationship? And if you have to be honest, do you think that it is fun to be around you? If not, do some soul searching to see where your joy has gone and what you can do to rekindle it.

Application:

Plan a memorable date for your spouse. Consider incorporating as many things that they like as possible, especially the small things that only you probably know.

Summer Day 9: Camping

The Lord said to Moses, "Say to the Israelites: 'On the fifteenth day of the seventh month the Lord's Festival of Tabernacles begins, and it lasts for seven days. The first day is a sacred assembly; do no regular work. For seven days present food offerings to the Lord, and on the eighth day hold a sacred assembly and present a food offering to the Lord. It is the closing special assembly; do no regular work."

Leviticus 23:33-36 (NIV)

Celebrating the Festival of Tabernacles

"The Feast of Booths (known to some as the Feast of Tabernacles) is the seventh and last festival on the biblical calendar, as recorded in Leviticus 23. Also known as Sukkot in Hebrew, God wanted the Israelites to observe this festival by living in temporary shelters for seven days as a reminder that when their ancestors were in the wilderness, God provided them booths to dwell in," (Zimmerman, 2015).

The first time the Bible speaks of Jehovah Jireh is in Genesis 22, when God provided Abraham with a ram to be sacrificed in place of Isaac. It is with this dramatic save that God introduced us to this element of His character.

We see that, through the installation and celebration of the Festival of Tabernacles, God wants us to honor

Him when He provides for us and to remember how He has come through for us in the past.

Constant worrying is something that can wreck a marriage. Because it is so easy to allow anxiety and stress to make us forget about how faithful God is, we continuously need to remind each other that God is for us and that His plans for us are good.

Prayer:

Thank You, Lord, for providing for our needs. You have never failed us. Forgive us when we forget about Your faithfulness, when our mind limits Your power, and when we think our own plans are better than Yours.

Reflection:

Do you believe the following verse: "For I know the plans I have for you," declares the Lord, "plans to prosper you and not to harm you, plans to give you hope and a future," Jeremiah 29:11 (NIV)? If not, consider your opinion of Father God. How do you see him? Does your view of Him align with who He really is, or have you allowed circumstances and people to influence and tarnish the way you see Him?

Application:

Make a working list that you constantly add to when God comes through for you—in big or small ways. When doubt, stress, or anxiety want to rear their ugly head, take the list and remind yourself of who your God is and what He is capable of. Tell yourself that His timing is perfect even when it feels like you're entering the eleventh hour.

Also, make a point of respecting the Fifth Commandment and having a day of rest. Being well rested gives perspective to a lot of life's complications.

Summer Day 10: Black-Eyed Susans

… they heap abuse on you. But they will have to give an account
to Him who is ready to judge the living and the dead.

I Peter 4:4b-5 (BSB)

Abuse in a Marriage

Black-eyed susans are cheerful summer flowers. They cover their surroundings with a beautiful hue of yellow. In the language of the flowers, black-eyed susans represent justice.

During a Google search to verify a scripture reference, I typed in the word 'husband' and Google did its thing by providing the most searched topics starting with my search term. The top hit immediately caught my attention: "husband sexually abuses me." For a while I simply just stared at the screen. How is it possible for that to be the most searched phrase starting with the word 'husband'?

It reminded me of a sermon I watched on YouTube where a pastor looks out over his congregation and lists abuse statistics. He takes it a step further to mention that if the statistics are accurate, then around 60 of the women sitting in the room are being abused by their husbands (Slager, 2018). He makes a beautiful plea to the women to come find help because that is not how God intended for marriage to be.

I know it sounds like I'm picking on husbands here—I'm not! I am all too aware of the statistics where wives are the abusers. I have a friend who had to flee his marriage because his petite, five foot something wife had a short temper and an affinity for big knives.

The point I am trying to make is that abuse—sexual, verbal, mental, and emotional—has perverted marriages, and that we should take up the call to show the world what a godly marriage looks like. I'm not talking about a perfect marriage, they don't exist. I'm talking about a marriage where both partners love, trust, respect, and honor each other. Where the children born from that union have the correct view of what God wants a marriage to be.

Marriage is fundamental to society. A healthy marriage is the cornerstone of a healthy society.

Prayer:

Jesus, help us to show the world what a godly marriage looks like. Help us to stay rooted in You so that we can produce the life-giving fruit of the Spirit.

Reflection:

The world needs to see what a marriage is meant to be. Consider which couples you look to as inspiration for your marriage. What exactly do you see in their relationship that speaks so clearly to your definition of marriage? Is it possible for your marriage to be the example that another couple needs for their marriage to improve?

Application:

Root yourselves in the Word. Plug yourself into the Vine.

Note: There are people willing to help if you are trapped in an abusive marriage. Please, please reach out to them.

Summer Day 11: Gone Fishing

And Jesus said unto them, "Come ye after me, and I will make you to become fishers of men."

Mark 1:17 (KJV)

The Catch

I grew up fishing. It can yield many a great reward. It forces you to slow down and appreciate what is around you. It grants you the time to connect with friends and family as you sit next to the water waiting for a bite.

The rewards of being a fisher of men are even greater—you can change a person's life and destiny.

Jesus was very clear when He gave us the Great Commission in Matthew 28.

> "Therefore go and make disciples of all nations, baptizing them in the name of the Father and of the Son and of the Holy Spirit, and teaching them to obey everything I have commanded you. And surely I am with you always, to the very end of the age," (Matthew 28:19-20, NIV).

What's more is that He doesn't choose a specific group of people to commit to the commission. It is something that everyone has to do: those who are single, those who are married, the young, the old, recent converts, mature believers—every single one of us.

Prayer:

Father, Your love for Your creation is immense, strong, passionate, fierce, and unconditional. It must be difficult to stand back and watch how your children self-destruct. Create in me a heart that beats for your children, Lord, and the desire to seek the lost and hungry.

Finally, let me borrow the words of Matthew West's song, *My Own Little World* (2010):

"Break my heart for what breaks yours

Give me open hands and open doors

Put your light in my eyes and let me see

That my own little world is not about me".

Reflection:

You and your spouse are called to make disciples and share the Gospel with them. How have you incorporated the Great Commission into your marriage?

Application:

Ask the Lord to show you the people in your life that He wants you to influence, minister to, or make disciples of.

Summer Day 12: Long Days

Yes, you will suffer for a short time. But after that, God will make everything right. He will make you strong. He will support you and keep you from falling. He is the God who gives all grace. He chose you to share in his glory in Christ. That glory will continue forever. All power is his forever. Amen.

I Peter 5:10-11 (ERV)

Hold Fast, Your Breakthrough is Coming

Because earth is tilted towards the sun during summer, the days seem longer due to the increased amount of direct sunlight that shines down on whichever hemisphere is experiencing summer.

Similarly, when we are going through a difficult patch, time feels slower, days feel longer.

We were warned that life on earth is not always going to be fun and games. "I have said these things to you, that in me you may have peace. In the world you will have tribulation. But take heart; I have overcome the world," (John 16:33, ESV). But we were also given the assurance that good has already triumphed. And if we continue to do what is right, in spite of our circumstances, the reward will be great. "So let's not get tired of doing what is good. At just the right time we will reap a harvest of blessing if we don't give up," (Galatians 6:9, NLT).

I realize that these words may sound hollow, like I make light of your tough situation, your dire circumstances, when the truth is that I know exactly how it is to feel forsaken and alone. Rejected by the ones who say that they will be there, regardless. But I can also share a lesson my experience with God has taught me: He is a faithful God. He has never failed me.

Your spouse is one of the most precious gifts you can have during times of trouble. A friend once told me that a marriage is a wheel, when the one is at the bottom. the other is able to pull them up.

Prayer:

Father, sustain me during times of trial. Remind me of how blessed I am, how strong I am in You, and how faithful You are. Send the correct people over my path so that I may draw strength and wisdom from them.

Reflection:

This too shall pass. Are you holding on to the belief that your breakthrough is coming, or have your circumstances stolen your joy? What has caused you to believe that?

Application:

If your marriage partner is going through a tough time, rearrange your schedule so that you have enough time to support and pray for them. Be a shoulder they can cry on, an ear that will listen, and a heart that will understand.

If you are the one who is facing immense struggles, spend more time in the presence of the Lord. He will give you what you need to carry on. Be open with your spouse, especially about your needs. Allow them to help carry you through the darker times.

Summer Day 13: Footsteps in The Sand

*The Lord of hosts is with us; The God of Jacob is our stronghold.
Selah.*

Psalm 46:7 (ESV)

You are Not Alone

Marriage can be a lonely place, especially if there is only one of you looking to keep it alive. It is during these worst-of-the-worst kind of times that you will see the faithfulness of the Lord.

This poem has been doing the rounds for quite some time now. At one stage you could find it everywhere—on mugs, t-shirts, calendars, you name it. And while this is true and you probably know this poem as well as me, it doesn't take away from how profound the poem really is.

One night I dreamed a dream.

As I was walking along the beach with my Lord.

Across the dark sky flashed scenes from my life.

For each scene, I noticed two sets of footprints in the sand,

One belonging to me and one to my Lord.

After the last scene of my life flashed before me,

I looked back at the footprints in the sand.

I noticed that at many times along the path of my life,

especially at the very lowest and saddest times,

there was only one set of footprints.

This really troubled me, so I asked the Lord about it.

"Lord, you said once I decided to follow you,

You'd walk with me all the way.

But I noticed that during the saddest and most
troublesome times of my life,

there was only one set of footprints.

I don't understand why, when I needed You the most,
You would leave me."

He whispered, "My precious child, I love you and will
never leave you

Never, ever, during your trials and testings.

When you saw only one set of footprints,

It was then that I carried you."

—Margaret Fishback Powers

Prayer:

Beloved Father, thank You for always being there for
me; for carrying me during the worst parts of my life;
for sustaining me when I wanted to give up.

Reflection:

"Be strong and courageous. Do not fear or be in dread of them, for it is the LORD your God who goes with you. He will not leave you or forsake you," (Deuteronomy 31:6, ESV).

Application:

As emotions tend to cloud judgment, you need to remind yourself of the truth during times when emotions run high. Compile a list of scriptures you can memorize and subsequently recite for times when you feel alone, powerless, or afraid. There is a reason why the Bible features as a sword in our spiritual armor (see Ephesians 6).

Summer Day 14: Pineapple

"There is a boy here who has five barley loaves and two fish, but what are they for so many?"

John 6:9 (ESV)

Starting Small

Many, many moons ago, I went on a mission trip to the Congo. While it was an incredibly challenging and piercing time in my life, it was also filled with profound and revelatory moments.

During this trip, I had the opportunity to be part of something both life-changing and life-giving: Preparing a field so that we can plant pineapple tops in the hope that it will produce a healthy, bountiful harvest of the golden fruits.

We dug, we tilled, and we planted in the hot African sun. When my group of volunteers stepped back at the end of the process, we rejoiced. The image of the green pineapple crown, standing small but tall, reaching out to the heavens and starting to create roots, spoke about God's goodness and what can be accomplished when we partner with Him.

I never saw those pineapples grow, what they had to endure to mature, or the final phase of harvesting, but I know that I did my part. The rest wasn't up to me. It was up to the others that were there for the rest of that season, as well as Father God Himself.

If you are in a difficult place in your marriage, how appropriate is the symbol of a pineapple! It is not an 'easy' fruit. You can't just bite into it. There is a painful process involved to get to the sweet and juicy flesh.

Bring any brokenness to the Lord, whatever is left of your heart or your marriage. Plant it as an act of faith. Do your part, and then stand back so that God can do the rest. Keep listening to His voice, and do what He asks. Your harvest might just astound you.

The fact is, it is the small things that make a big difference.

Prayer:

Holy Spirit, please make my soul sensitive to the small things I can do to bless my spouse. And help me recognize and appreciate the small things they do to make my life better.

Reflection:

"Sometimes the smallest things take up the most room in your heart," —Winnie the Pooh.

What are the small things that you appreciate so much about your marriage partner? Do you acknowledge and thank your spouse for them when necessary?

Application:

Commit to doing at least one little thing each day that will bless your spouse, like making them a cup of coffee, running them a bath, watching a documentary with them that they enjoy, et cetera.

Chapter 3:

Autumn

Autumn whispered to the wind, "I fall; but always rise again."

—Angie Weiland-Crosby

Autumn Day 1: Have You Started Your Winter Preparations?

Bear one another's burdens, and so fulfill the law of Christ.

Galatians 6:2 (ESV)

Accountability Partners

During autumn, many an animal and person start preparing for the winter months ahead. The animals have a powerful instinct and drive to guide them. As human beings, we have the humans that went before us to guide and drive us to do the things we need to do.

Inherently, human beings are lovers of short-cuts so we take what worked for others and simplify it. We love calling it being effective, productive, or frugal. Sometimes these approaches are exactly what the situation calls for, but then there are times when a shortcut simply won't do. Take marriage or finances as examples. Short-cuts don't work well here.

In cases such as these, it is important to have an accountability partner who is wise enough to mentor us as we face difficulties and unknown challenges. However, accountability partners take things a step further than just giving advice. They check up on us to see if we are walking the walk and not only talking the talk, since it is just too easy to break a promise or take a short-cut. And let's be honest, sometimes this is exactly what we need.

Prayer:

Father God, making a marriage work between two imperfect beings can seem like an impossible job. Thank You for supplying us with loving mentors who are willing to help us on this road we are on. Help me to take the time to listen to them, measure what they say against the Word, and do the right thing.

Reflection:

Marriage should be too important to us to try to go it alone. What is stopping you from reaching out to other believers and asking them for help or advice?

Application:

Invite a godly accountability partner into your life. Try to find someone who has a spouse with a similar disposition as yours as it will help you understand your spouse so much better.

Autumn Day 2: Apple Picking

"My lover is an apple tree, the finest in the orchard as compared with any of the other youths. I am seated in his much-desired shade and his fruit is lovely to eat."

Song of Solomon 2:3 (TLB)

My Lover

An apple tree is so much more than an apple tree. Yes, that is its basic description and for all intents and purposes—it is an apple tree, but upon closer inspection, more can be found there.

It is a home to many creatures, while providing shelter to others during storms or chases. It provides a shadow to the weary during the heat of the day. Its fruit can be eaten and its wood can be burned.

In a similar fashion, we can't simply attach a singular meaning to the word 'lover'. I remember hearing it as a child and having my cheeks flame up with embarrassment. Obviously, I only associated the word with sex.

Your lover is your sexual partner, but they are also your home, your protection, your nourishment. They offer you

- their calm during one of your storms
- their arms during your sadness

- their strength during your weakness
- their acceptance and love during your loneliness
- their body as your comfort
- their hope during a time of despair

Prayer:

Father, help me to show my lover my appreciation for all that they offer me. Help me to meet their needs as well. Remind me to draw from Your strength and wisdom so that
I don't attempt these things on my own.

Reflection:

A lover is one of the biggest blessings you will ever be given. Is this how you see your partner? Or yourself? If not, explore the reasons.

Application:

Have a conversation with your spouse and ask them about their expectation and definition of what a lover is. Ask each other if there are ways to improve to better meet each other's needs.

Autumn Day 3: The Leaves are Falling

The grass withers, the flower fades, but the word of our God will stand forever.

Isaiah 40:8 (ESV)

The Decline

While autumn is a beautiful season with its rich colors and sweet smells—my favorite season by far—it is also a season marked by decline. The trees lose their leaves, the plants die, the days lose their warmth and length…

If we consider that people in general get married between the ages of 25 and 30, we realize that much of the life we spend together features decline.

After 30 our hair starts graying, our face starts to wrinkle, our metabolism slows down, our vitality decreases, et cetera. And while these things are not optimal for our youth-driven society, these things don't matter so much in the greater scheme of things. Marriage is about growing old together and facing whatever physical decline comes our way.

Growing old together, however, also means getting to know each other better, sharing beautiful moments with each other, bringing life into the world, not being alone any more—the list is endless.

Prayer:

Give me your eyes, dear Lord, so that I may see my marriage spouse through Your eyes. Help me to celebrate each wrinkle, gray hair, and creaking joint as it all forms part of the incredible journey we get to walk together.

Reflection:

We need to reframe our mindsets when it comes to facing natural decline. For example, the Word reads in Proverbs 16:31 (NIV), that "Gray hair is a crown of splendor." How do you feel about aging? Are you positive or negative about it?

Application:

Actively reject the standards of the times you are living in. These standards of eternal youth, immediate pleasure, discarding relationships and responsibilities, go against God's will for us. Instead, celebrate your spouse and each milestone they reach, like you would do for a child. Every milestone is precious.

Autumn Day 4: Pumpkins Versus Jack-O'-Lanterns

Moreover, it is required of stewards that they be found trustworthy.

I Corinthians 4:2 (ESV)

Using Resources Wisely

One of the signature images of the autumn season will always be pumpkins. It appears in so many different forms and dishes.

While I love a beautifully carved pumpkin, there is a part of me that wants to cringe at the sight of a "wasted" pumpkin. The part that wants to criticize that particular use of a food is the part that is all too aware of how much hunger there is in the world. The little voice in my head will cry, "That pumpkin could have fed a family of six." It is also the voice that doesn't like using macaroni in art projects, or popcorn as tree decor.

While I have to tone down that part of me at times because I recognize the need for the joy that a jack-o'-lantern, macaroni project, or popcorn garland brings, it can't help but raise the question if we invest our resources in the best possible way.

God wants us to be good stewards of that which He has blessed us with. He says that He will reward us with more, if we are found to be faithful with the little things He bestows on us (Luke 6:10). Yet God doesn't tell us what 'faithful' looks like. This means that resource distribution could be a huge matter of contention in a marriage as your priorities may differ. In matters such as these, especially where one spouse feels really strongly about certain things, compromise can seem like a pipe dream.

What God is very clear about in His Word is unity, love, and respect. If that can be the basis of any conversation regarding finances, assets, or pumpkins, then the conversation will probably end in a successful conclusion.

Prayer:

Thank You, Father, for all our blessings. You are a good and generous God. Help us to be good stewards of what You have provided. Help us to give each other grace when we feel differently about how to use or distribute our resources.

Reflection:

"Do not store up for yourselves treasures on earth, where moths and vermin destroy, and where thieves break in and steal. But store up for yourselves treasures in heaven, where moths and vermin do not destroy, and where thieves do not break in and steal. For where your treasure is, there your heart will be also," (Matthew 6:19-21, NIV).

Where would you say your priorities lie?

Application:

Have budget-related conversations when and where there is a peaceful atmosphere, preferably on neutral ground. Listen to each other's ideas and carefully consider them.

Ask whether what you choose to spend your money on, has a Kingdom component, something with value that is everlasting that will build or edify the body. This isn't necessarily as heavy as what it sounds. Sometimes this takes the shape of a much needed family vacation where you get to reconnect and affirm relationships; other times this could look like a donation to a charity.

Autumn Day 5: Sweaters

Is anyone among you in trouble? Let them pray.

James 5:13a (NIV)

The Protection of Prayer

As autumn matures and the cold starts its ever so subtle take-over of the air around us, we are quick to grab something with long sleeves to protect us against the chill. What beautiful relief the warmth brings our shivering bodies.

When trouble first appears on the horizon, our default is often not what it should be. The ladies like to huddle together, sometimes inviting a glass of wine or a pint of ice cream to the gathering. The men like to suppress their emotions, sometimes even deny the existence of the problem—until there is an eruption of sorts. Neither way of dealing with the issue at hand is successful. It is like grabbing a single sock when you feel cold. It does very little to solve the problem.

What we should be doing is taking the matter, first and foremost, to the Lord. He wants to be our solid rock in times of trouble. Philippians 4:6 (BSB) tells us to "[b]e anxious for nothing, but in everything, by prayer and petition, with thanksgiving, present your requests to God."

Prayer is a powerful force. We get to empty our hearts in a safe and loving space. Neuroscientist Caroline Leaf coined the phrase "freaking out in the love-zone" and I find it very applicable here.

Opening up like this to our Heavenly Father protects us and our marriages in many ways. Oftentimes we are the one who is in the wrong, and not our spouse. By going to friends or family with our troubles, we give them a one-sided interpretation of events. With the inaccurate facts we give them, we cast our spouse in an unfairly negative light. The advice given is not always the best, if the conversation is limited to advice since it often turns to petty mud-slinging.

Prayer:

Father, since You are the only one who knows all things, help me to turn to You when things get tough in my marriage. Help me to understand what is truly happening and show me where my thoughts, attitudes, words, and actions are contributing to the difficulties my spouse and I go through. Help me to forgive my spouse and look forward to what lies ahead.

Reflection:

"Prayer is essential for a vibrant relationship with God and it's just as vital for a healthy, vibrant marriage" — Fiercemarriage.com.

How much time do you spend talking to the Lord? Would you say that you have a healthy prayer life?

Application:

Draw up a game-plan for yourself of how you will deal with any issues that arise in your marriage. Writing it down makes it easier to follow. Remember to list the first step as "Go to the Lord." If you prefer, you could do this activity as a couple.

Autumn Day 6: A-peel-ing Apples

And the LORD God said, "It is not good that man should be alone; I will make him a helper comparable to him."

Genesis 2:18 (NKJV)

The Woman and Wife

Apples are often compared to women, whether it is in regards to shape, flavor, quality, variety, or texture. Apart from that, it is a fruit that is extremely beneficial to women specifically. Eating apples regularly lowers cholesterol and blood fat levels, it decreases the risk of developing chronic diseases such as cancer, heart disease, and diabetes, while potentially boosting weightloss, digestion, gut health, mental health, and sexual pleasure.

My favorite of this wonder fruit is the Granny Smith Apple, my go-to for all needs that are apple-related. I love their shiny, green exterior, their firm flesh and, rather tart-like flavor. I appreciate that their sweetness is brought out either through a long period of storage or with heat. It reminds me of the process we, as women, undergo on our journey of maturation.

An apple starts off connected to a tree, drawing its nourishment from its branches. It grows into what God intended it to be: a sustaining, live-giving force. After it is picked from the tree, it is washed and packed by a manufacturer. There the fate of an apple varies: some are used for juice, some are canned, some are dried, and some are sold as is.

What is interesting, is that all these apples will undergo hardships to bring out the aromas and flavors that God wants in the world. Being chopped, squeezed, cooked, and dried are not my idea of a good time. As women, these translate to the difficulties we face daily while wearing our different hats.

I am a wife, mother, daughter, friend, coach, and business owner. Each of these hats bring their own challenges and trials. Each brings their own rewards and benefits.

Prayer:

Wife - Father God, give me the grace and courage I need every day. Thank You for always being there when life is tough and I am swamped with household chores, work responsibilities, and relational issues.

Husband - Lord God, thank You for my wife. Help me to be a good husband to her that she may see Jesus in me. Help me to support her in all she undertakes with love and understanding.

Reflection:

And they lived happily ever after exists only in fairy tales we as women love to read, but that doesn't mean that your life will be unfulfilled or unhappy. Is there something keeping you from creating a more joyful life?

Application:

Ladies, try to embrace your journey, every part of it. It has a lot to do with having a growth mindset. A growth mindset has to do with seeing the potential of every situation you come across, and translating the potential into success. Then when the tests come, you will pass them and when the trials come, you will overcome them.

Gentlemen, support and love your wives through the ups and downs of her journey. She needs you more than you realize.

Autumn Day 7: Black Friday

Only fear the Lord and serve Him faithfully with all your heart.
For consider what great things He has done for you.

I Samuel 12:24 (ESV)

Those Special Moments

For people who are in need of something and on a very limited budget, Black Friday is a big deal, literally and figuratively. There has been a time or two when my family and I walked away with so much more than our money would normally have been able to purchase.

It reminds me of the gracious nature of our Father in Heaven. He surpasses our dues time and time again. His economy is not our economy.

When approaching our life partner, we should mimic God's generosity in every area of marriage.

I know a lady who wrote out a list dividing the household responsibilities between her and her then husband. Both of them were responsible for 50% of the tasks. In her mind it made perfect sense: 50% plus 50% equals a 100% marriage arrangement. While the math made sense on paper, it did not translate into real life.

He would come home at night, after a very trying day at work, to find that she did not make food for him. Dinner was his responsibility. She already did her 50%.

I learned a very important lesson from the break-up of their marriage. If we want a 100% marriage, both spouses need to give 100%, picking up the slack when the other is unable to. This is exactly what the Lord does for us.

Prayer:

Lord God, please help me to give of myself in my marriage the way You gave Yourself for me. Stop me when I try to calculate perceived efforts just so that my spouse will come up short.

Reflection:

"Do all the good you can,

By all the means you can,

In all the ways you can,

In all the places you can,

At all the times you can,

To all the people you can,

As long as ever you can" —John Wesley

Have you got a 50% or a 100% mindset when it comes to serving in a marriage?

Application:

Create special moments for your spouse just to remind them that you are 100% committed to your marriage and that you are willing to give it 100% to make it successful.

Autumn Day 8: Wanted: Cranberry Sauce!

Sweet friendships refresh the soul and awaken our hearts with joy, for good friends are like the anointing oil that yields the fragrant incense of God's presence.

Proverbs 27:9 (TPT)

Friends

Cranberries are often associated with autumn. In fact, after pumpkins and apples, it is probably the season's third most favored flavor. No decent Thanksgiving table will ever be seen without it.

For Thanksgiving last year, my table almost didn't feature any cranberry sauce. And it wasn't for lack of trying. I went to every store within a 30-mile radius of my house. Nothing! Nada! Not even a lone piece of cranberry sauce packaging could be seen anywhere. Finally, with hope almost turned to despair, I phoned a friend. She had two cans that she could give me. Thanksgiving was saved.

How often do we go on crazed solo missions trying to fix, fulfill, and find things. We spend so much time and energy "out there" when the answer is closer to home.

This experience reminded me about the precious people God placed in my life. Wise and wonderful people who walk with me. They take the form of my husband, family members, and faithful friends and neighbors.

Prayer:

Lord, thank You for the strategic people that You have placed in my life. You know my journey well, You know who and what I need, and You have already made provision for that. Help me to wait upon You when troubles arise and not try to go it alone. Clearly show me which friend I should reach out to. Also give me the courage to step out and be vulnerable with them.

Reflection:

"Anything is possible when you have the right people there to support you" —Misty Copeland.

How do you handle a season of need? Are you the type of person who gratefully accepts help?

Application:

When God places someone on your heart, reach out to them. They could be just who you need for where you currently find yourself. Or the converse may be true, you could be who they need.

Autumn Day 9: Don't *Leaf* Me—You Said You'll Catch Me When I *Fall*

For everything there is a season,

A time for every activity under heaven.

A time to be born and a time to die.

A time to plant and a time to harvest.

A time to kill and a time to heal.

A time to tear down and a time to build up.

A time to cry and a time to laugh.

A time to grieve and a time to dance.

A time to scatter stones and a time to gather stones.

A time to embrace and a time to turn away.

A time to search and a time to quit searching.

A time to keep and a time to throw away.

A time to tear and a time to mend.

A time to be quiet and a time to speak.

A time to love and a time to hate.

A time for war and a time for peace.

Ecclesiastes 3:1-8 (NLT)

For Richer and Poorer, In Sickness and In Health

What a corny autumn pun to introduce a serious topic: choosing to stay together when the tough times come. And they will. In fact, Jesus guaranteed it in John 16:33 (NLT), "Here on earth you will have many trials and sorrows." It is foolish to believe otherwise. However, the verse does not end there. The verse ends with our Savior declaring, "But take heart, because I have overcome the world."

It is God's will that we prosper in every area of our life as can be seen in 3 John 1:2 (KJV), "Beloved, I wish above all things that thou mayest prosper and be in health, even as thy soul prospereth." But He is more concerned with our character than our comforts, so He allows difficulties to come so that our roots will shoot deeper into Him.

Finances

A good friend of mine always used to say that money is a thought. And while I wish that statement was literal— I'm an over-thinker so I would be a multimillionaire, adding to my networth daily—the statement implies that money has a transient nature.

The stress and anxiety that can be caused, by both money and the lack thereof, is monumental and is rooted in fear. To the Lord it looks like we're telling him, "I don't think You have this." How insulting. Yes, He is not dealing with the situation the way we might want Him to, but as the creation, not the Creator, are we more capable to handle the situation than our Omnipotent, Omnipresent, Omnibenevolent, and Omniscient God? I think not.

It is so important to stand united and hold fast to the promises in the Word, especially when the storms are raging around us. Make sure you don't allow money, in any form, to come between you and your spouse. Instead, You made a vow to each other to be there, regardless of what is happening in the bank.

Health and Wellbeing

Sickness is very taxing on those it impacts, whether it is the one that is unwell or their friends, family, or loved ones. It has the capacity to break us physically, mentally, and spiritually. Like finances, it can, and all too frequently does, rip families apart.

Physical trauma does funny things to people. It can cause us to shut down, build walls, retaliate, and give up. But it can also bring people together, make us stronger, make us smarter, and help us to see what really matters in this world. It all has to do with perspective.

Earth is not our true home. It is simply where we get to choose where we want to spend eternity and grow in the knowledge of our heavenly Father, Jesus Christ, and the Holy Spirit. However big our challenges seem, they aren't. Not even death is as bad as it feels—it is our journey to our true home.

Prayer:

Lord, help us to stick together during the trials that life brings us. May we be like Paul and Silas. May You find us worshiping in the worst of circumstances.

Reflection:

"And we know [with great confidence] that God [who is deeply concerned about us] causes all things to work together [as a plan] for good for those who love God, to those who are called according to His plan and purpose," (Romans 8:28, AMP). Are you able to worship during the worst of times because you know, that you know, that you know that God is a loving Father who has good plans for His children?

Application:

When things get bad, force yourself to not see your spouse as the enemy. Even if it may not look like it, they are on the same side as you. Remember who the true enemy is and that one of his master plans is misdirection. He wants us to be fully consumed with each other so that we don't target him and cut him off at the knees.

Don't lose hope, even if things seem hopeless.

Financially, do what is expected of you as seen in the Word, tithing and giving freely, Remember that God's economy does not look like yours.

Honor your body as the temple of the Holy Spirit. Make healthy choices for you and your family.

Autumn Day 10: Harvests

Do not be deceived, God is not mocked; for whatever a man sows, that he will also reap. For he who sows to his flesh will of the flesh reap corruption, but he who sows to the Spirit will of the Spirit reap everlasting life. And let us not grow weary while doing good, for in due season we shall reap if we do not lose heart.

Galatians 6:7-9 (NKJV)

You Reap What You Sow

Autumn is synonymous with harvesting. It is the time of year when farmers get to gather, examine, and sell whatever it is they planted.

A few basic principles exist when it comes to sowing and reaping. The most obvious one is that you will reap what you sow.

The question is, when it comes to your marriage, what are you sowing? Do you sow healthy, life-giving seeds, like faithfulness, generosity, positivity, joy, love, hope, and kindness? Or can you be found, more often than not, planting anger, greed, abuse, negativity, and hostility into the fertile ground of your marriage?

If you are unsure of the type of seeds you are sowing, examine your harvest. One of the most brutal ways of doing this is asking your spouse to tell you what they experience in your marriage.

If you are dissatisfied with your harvest, it is time to change your seed.

Verse 9 in today's scripture encourages us to continue doing good when it is hard to do so; to carry on being the spouse God wants us to be when your spouse is not keeping up their side of the bargain. It promises us that we will reap a glorious harvest if we don't give up and walk away.

Prayer:

Jesus, Savior, You know how fickle human beings can be. How easy it is for us not to do the right thing and hurt our loved ones. Help us, in accordance with Ephesians 4:22, to put off our old self, which belongs to our previous way of life and is corrupted with deceitful desires, and be renewed in Christ, and to put on our new self, created in the image of God in true righteousness and holiness. May we sow seeds of life and be a blessing to our spouse.

Reflection:

"Life is an echo. What you send out, comes back. What you sow, you reap. What you give, you get. What you see in others, exists in you" —Zig Ziglar.

When you look at what you sow into your marriage, what do you, realistically, expect your harvest to be?

Application:

As mentioned in the devotional entry earlier, more specifically *Autumn Day 6: A-peeling Apples*, ask your spouse about the type of seeds they see you sowing in your marriage. Even if it is uncomfortable, the truth will provide you with a strategy of what needs to be changed in order to make your marriage a healthier place.

Autumn Day 11: Goldenrod

Therefore encourage one another and build each other up...

I Thessalonians 5:11 (NIV)

Encourage One Another

Goldenrods don't self-pollinate. They have to draw a lot of bees and butterflies to their wispy yellow blooms for cross pollination to occur. Due to the fact that they hold such a mass appeal for bees, and the fact that goldenrods produce so much nectar, they are invaluable when it comes to the production of honey.

Humans were also not created to be an island of self-sufficiency. This is why solitary confinement in prisons is one of the harshest punishments imposed on prisoners. We need others to survive.

A big reason why we need the presence of others is because of the encouragement factor. Loved ones encourage us to grow, learn, let go, hold on, and move forward..

Are you a source of encouragement to your spouse? Do you inspire them to reach new heights, chase their dream, or be brave enough to show their true self to the world?

Or do they dread the time when you walk through the door? Are they, metaphorically speaking, slowly dying under your critical gaze?

Prayer:

Jesus, help me to be more like You. Help me to bring life to my spouse with my words and actions. May I never become so focussed on my needs, dreams, and desires that I forsake to do what You have called me to do—encourage and build up my spouse.

Reflection:

How you make others feel about themselves says a lot about you. Have you thought about how others feel when they are in your presence? Do you build or break those around you?

Application:

When you find yourself ready to critique your spouse, ask yourself if that is what they truly need at that moment. If they are in a position to receive the critique in a positive, life-enhancing way, then have that conversation with them.

If they are not in a good place, and what you want to say will not benefit them, then choose to give them a word of encouragement. As the saying goes: *It is better to be kind than to be right.*

Autumn Day 12: Autumn Blush Coreopsis

Not that I speak from want, for I have learned to be content in whatever circumstances I am. I know how to get along with humble means, and I also know how to live in prosperity; in any and every circumstance I have learned the secret of being filled and going hungry, both of having abundance and suffering need. I can do all things through Him who strengthens me.

Philippians 4:11-13 (NASB)

Walter Mitty

I will never be able to see the word 'coreopsis' without thinking of *The Secret Life of Walter Mitty*. I am not talking about the movie starring Ben Stiller and Kirsten Wiig, I mean the short story written by James Thurber in 1939.

Walter Jackson Mitty would have been a very forgettable character, had it not been for his incredible flights of fancy. During one of his fantastical adventures, Mitty imagines himself to be a renowned medical specialist who is called upon to save a friend of the president. No one else but Mitty can do the job because "[c]oreopsis has set in." For the layman it may not mean much, but for any expert in flora, it would mean a very serious question mark.

Coreopsis is a very common flower, not a medical term.

Walter Jackson Mitty is a weak character completely dominated by his overbearing wife. In order to make his life a little more bearable, he imagines himself to be various fearless, dynamic heroes who ooze with charm and charisma. Due to the fact that he is not an expert in anything, he uses vocabulary that sounds impressive but is completely (and comically) incorrect in the given context.

Do you do something similar? Do you prefer living in your head where things are better and you are always on the top of the game? Or maybe technology is your great escape? It might not even be an escapist issue. It could be that you are addicted to overthinking. If any of these are featured in your life, you may be making it very hard for your spouse to fully connect with you.

In the language of flowers, the coreopsis bloom means "always cheerful" and that is what we have to choose to be. "This is the day that the Lord has made; let us rejoice and be glad in it," (Philippians 4:11-13.) We need to focus on our blessings as well as being content when we are in a season of waiting on the Lord.

Prayer:

Lord, help me to be present during the times I am with my spouse. Help me to see when I allow distractions to take priority because I do not want to deal with my reality.

Reflection:

To be content doesn't mean you don't desire more, it means you're thankful for what you have and patient for what is to come," —Tony Gaskins.

How accurately does this quote describe you?

Application:

Institute practices, such as switching off distracting devices, during important family times, like dinners or dates, so that your spouse will not receive mixed messages regarding the desirability of your life together.

Autumn Day 13: Pomegranates

Behold, children are a heritage from the Lord, the fruit of the womb a reward.

Psalm 127:3 (ESV)

The Fruit of Your Womb

Pomegranates "provides a powerhouse of heart-healthy antioxidants, lycopene, potassium, and fiber making it an excellent fall food choice," (Rellinger, 2012).

The Old Testament contains many references to pomegranates. They were a favored symbol used in the garments of the high priests and both the tabernacle and temple. When specifically focussing on Numbers 13:23 and Deuteronomy 8:8, pomegranates symbolize fruitfulness, blessing, and prosperity.

More and more couples are deciding not to have children. I respect their decision because raising kids is one of the hardest things in the world. And regardless of how much we read up beforehand, or who we consult, nothing prepares us for it.
Then there's also the fact that as soon as we conquer one phase, another one starts throwing us back in the deep end.

But despite all the stretch marks, tears, and financial implications, children are a blessing. The minute they place the baby in our arms and we get to glimpse the love that our Heavenly Father has for us, we're lost in wonder. I have often thought about how atheists can feel the way they do when there are the tiny hands and feet of a newborn to look at.

As parents, we have to point our kids to the Lord by making sure we embody all that He represents. This means raising our little ones with equal parts love and discipline.

When anger and frustration play too big a role, we need to be able to apologize and do serious self-examination. It is prudent to ask the Lord to heal any wounds that exist and are triggered by the children before a cycle is created and our behavior becomes their behavior.

Prayer:

Thank You, Father, for blessing us with children. They are one of the biggest miracles we have ever witnessed. Help us to be the best parent we possibly can be as we reflect Your nature to the children. Give us Your eyes, so that we can see them the way You do. Forgive us when we make mistakes. Show us how to rectify them and establish a relationship with our children that will stand the test of time (and puberty).

Reflection:

You were created for your children and they were created for you. There is a master plan at work, with a lot of iron sharpening iron. How do you handle situations where there is conflict between you and your children? Will equal parts love and discipline be found in the way you address them?

Application:

Work at maintaining a good relationship with your children. Extend the love, grace , and understanding that God continually showers you with.

Note: Parents, I feel it is imperative to mention that we should not judge other parents for the decisions they make. Whether they have a normal birth or a C-section; whether they breastfeed or not; whether they homeschool or not—theirs is a journey we don't have all the facts of. We are meant to support one another, not make an already tough road so much harder.

Autumn Day 14: Monkshood

They have venom like the venom of a serpent…

Psalm 58:4 (NKJV)

Toxicity in a Relationship

"Monkshood is a distinctive looking wildflower borne on shoulder high erect and sturdy stems. The common name for this plant comes from the hood-like sepal on the flower. The hood is thought to look like an old-fashioned cowl worn by monks… All parts of monkshood are poisonous, especially the roots and seeds, and the flowers if eaten. In the past, wolves and criminals were poisoned with an extract from the European wolfsbane Acontium lycoctonum," ("Monkshood | AACC.org", n.d.).

The term *toxic people* was first found in a book of the same name that was published back in 1995. The author and psychologist, Dr. Lilian Glass states that a toxic relationship is "any relationship [between people who] don't support each other, where there's conflict and one seeks to undermine the other, where there's competition, where there's disrespect and a lack of cohesiveness," (Glass, 1997).

As you can imagine, a toxic relationship is hell on earth. Unfortunately, at one time or another, we all add toxic elements to our relationships. Whether it's an inability to support our spouse, conflict we bring on, undermining your significant other, unhealthy competition, a lack of respect, discord, misprioritization, or allowing the wrong people to influence us, we all hurt our relationships.

According to 2 Timothy 1:7 (ESV), we know that we do something to curb the negativity that we bring to the table "for God gave us a spirit not of fear but of power and love and self-control." When we practice self-control and operate from a place of love, we change the atmosphere and effects of our approach to one another. We bring life and not death.

Prayer:

Holy Spirit, You were given to us to help us navigate our life on earth. Thank You, that we can rely on Your wisdom and instruction when it comes to our marriage. Help us to operate under Your influence when we deal with each other during tough times.

Reflection:

"Do the best you can until you know better. Then when you know better, do better," —Maya Angelou.

When you have learned about a healthier way to deal with situations, do you incorporate these strategies into your daily living or do you allow negative emotions to rule when circumstances overwhelm you?

Application:

When you wake up in the morning, invite the Holy Spirit into your day. Ask Him to guide you as you work with one of the most precious gifts in your life—your spouse.

Note: If your relationship is constantly toxic, it is necessary for you to seek help. Reach out to experts and people you trust that can facilitate a way forward, whether it means seeing a therapist or finding a way out.

Chapter 4:

Winter

"To appreciate the beauty of a snowflake, it is necessary to stand out in the cold."

—Aristotle

Winter Day 1: It's Cold!

Like the cold of snow in the time of harvest is a faithful messenger to those who send him, for he refreshes the soul of his masters.

Proverbs 25:13 (KJV)

Being Reliable

The cold air of winter can be very refreshing and invigorating after being cooped up in a deliciously warm room. We can count on the cold to wake us up and energize us like little else.

Someone who is faithful and dependable is also considered a breath of fresh air in today's world. People have become less and less concerned about being there for others. "I need to be there for me," they say. We know that we can trust them to do whatever will secure their happiness, fortune, and future.

Out of curiosity, do your spouse and those who know you best describe you as faithful and dependable? Can they count on you to come through for them or do they think that it's easier just to ask someone else?

Prayer:

Father, I want to be known as a faithful spouse in regards to both reliability and purity. Please give me the strength to see this decision through until the very end.

Reflection:

"Don't be reliable only when it is convenient," —
Rachel Wolchin.

Have you shown yourself to be faithful, even when
circumstances make it challenging?

Application:

Prove yourself to be dependable by honoring your
commitments, your promises, and your vows to your
marriage partner on a daily basis. If you say you will do
something, then do it.

Winter Day 2: Snow

But if we walk in the light, as He is in the light, we have fellowship with one another, and the blood of Jesus, His Son, cleanses us from all sin.

1 John 1:7 (NIV)

Jesus Washed Us White As Snow

A landscape covered in fresh snow is exquisite in its beauty. It also features a sense of calm and tranquility that few other vistas do.

I want you to picture something for me. Imagine that when you pray to ask for forgiveness, a white snow-like cover settles on you, where your easily identifiable features are completely covered. You don't resemble yourself anymore, instead you look like the snow with which you have just been enveloped in.

This is a metaphorical representation of what happens when we accept Jesus as our personal Savior and accept the pardon His death on the cross brings. We are cleansed and covered by the snow. We don't resemble our past self.

If our spouse gave their heart to the Lord and repented of their sins, then they have been sanctified. When we look at our forgiven spouse, we need to only see the snow. We cannot hold on to the past or what happened there.

Prayer:

Make me more like You, Lord. Help me to forgive my spouse and their transgressions because I want to be a true imitator of Christ.

Reflection:

If God has forgiven your spouse, you need to forgive them too. As Christians, we follow our Master's example, we don't think ourselves above His actions. In turn, we get to experience His full forgiveness when we forgive (see Matthew 6:14). Is there an area that you are holding back unforgiveness for your spouse?

Application:

Do this especially before partaking in Communion. Take some time to sit before the Lord and ask Him to bring to mind anyone you still need to forgive. Sometimes we need to daily forgive the people who badly hurt us.

Winter Day 3: Winter Sweat

"How fragrant your cologne,"

Song of Solomon 1:2a (TLB)

"The king lies on his bed, enchanted by the fragrance of my perfume,"

Song of Solomon 1:12 (TLB)

The Fragrance You Exude

People from warmer regions are often shocked at the amount they sweat during a subzero winter. There are a number of reasons for the perspiration: your environment, being overdressed, stress and anxiety, or there may be an underlying medical condition.

Sweat often has a pungent odor. And that odor is intensified when you don't want to bathe because you find the cold too overwhelming.

A friend of mine was raised in a house where sarcasm was featured strongly. It was very much part of the family's sense of humor. While inside the confines of their home, the sarcasm was appreciated for its wit, whereas outside their walls, it was misunderstood and found to be offensive and off putting. They lived in a rather small, more conservative town. The people were not bad, narrow-minded people. They valued respect and uplifting others. My friend had to realize that she had to reign in her sarcasm if she wanted to have a social life. She was open to their opinions and ways, and metaphorically speaking, changed the odor she was permeating.

Have you considered what you smell like to your spouse? And I'm not talking about a physical smell, although that is important too. I am talking about the fragrance of your being.

Prayer:

Jesus, may the fragrance that I exude bring You joy. May I always know my audience so that I may honor them with my behavior and speech.

Reflection:

Your fragrance, literal and figurative, should inspire connection and intimacy with your spouse. Do you attract your spouse? Do they like to be with you and bask in your presence? Or is there something about you that others find to be foul?

Application:

Go the extra mile for your spouse: put on the perfume/cologne they like because (a) you want them to find you attractive, and (b) you want them to know that you care about what they like.

Also, ask yourself about the scent you send into the world every day. Does it reflect Christ to the world? If not, make sure you are securely plugged into the Vine so that you are able to produce godly fruit and the enticing aroma that goes with it.

Winter Day 4: Frostbite

Never be lacking in zeal, but keep your spiritual fervor, serving the Lord. Be joyful in hope, patient in affliction, faithful in prayer.

Romans 12:11-12 (NIV)

Climbing Everest

Climbing a mountain like Everest takes a lot of preparation, dedication, and sacrifice. There are immense risks, and at least five climbers die trying to summit each year.

> "In 2008, a team led by anesthesiologist Paul Firth published an analysis in the British Medical Journal of 192 deaths among more than 14,000 Everest climbers and Sherpas between 1921 and 2006. Of that total, 59 percent of the deaths were attributable to trauma either from falls or hazards such as avalanches. In 14 percent of the cases, the bodies were never found so details are unknown. The remaining 27 percent are the most interesting ones, attributed to non-trauma causes like altitude illness and hypothermia," (Hutchinson, 2021).

The stakes are incredibly high and yet these climbers push through incredible odds to fulfill their dream.

Having a healthy, godly marriage should feature quite high on our priority list. Our dedication to seeing it being realized should equal or even surpass the fervor that the mountaineers have when it comes to summiting their next peak.

Unfortunately, the human race is famous for being obsessed with the self: self-seeking, self-absorbed, self-conceited, self-elevating, and selfish. Don't get me started on selfies!

Despite our obstacles, most of them found within ourselves, we should never tire in our efforts to sacrifice for such a worthy cause.

Prayer:

Father God, it is all too easy to forget how important it is to prioritize my spouse and my marriage. Help me to be selfless and mimic the example Jesus set for us.

Reflection:

"Marriage is not a simple love affair, it's an ordeal, and the ordeal is the sacrifice of ego to a relationship in which two have become one," —Joseph Campbell.

Are there areas where you tend to act selfishly in your marriage? Why is that?

Application:

Take some time and contemplate what it is that makes your marriage worth fighting for. List the reasons on a piece of paper. Refer back to it when situations, emotions, and self-importance threaten your desire to lay down your life for your spouse.

Winter Day 5: Bears

Love is patient and kind; love does not envy or boast; it is not arrogant or rude. It does not insist on its own way; it is not irritable or resentful; it does not rejoice at wrongdoing, but rejoices with the truth. Love bears all things, believes all things, hopes all things, endures all things. Love never ends...

I Corinthians 13:4-8 (ESV)

Perfect Love

"Depending on the time of year, type of bear, and location, bears may be active during winter. In some locations, bears are active year-round, while bears in other locations are not,"(Ben, 2019).

Love, like the bears, is not always an active presence in our lives. Where it is sometimes necessary for the bears to hibernate, it is disastrous when love takes a break from our lives.

Perfect love can be summed up in one word: unconditional. Read the verse again—it is the epitome of unconditional love. Funnily enough, romance is not featured in that description and I believe that it is because there is so much more to love than roses, chocolates, hearts, and kisses.

There are many distinguished examples of unconditional love found in the Word of God:

- David and Jonathan
- Elkanah and Hannah
- Hosea
- The father of the prodigal son
- Jesus Christ

If we extended the list to feature the people reading this page, would your name be featured here?

Prayer:

Jesus, create in me a heart that is able to love without condition. Where I fail, please show me how to access more of Your love so that I may fill up my tank and allow it to spill over to those around me.

Reflection:

Just as you want to be loved, your spouse wants to be loved too. How can you show your spouse your love for them in a new way today?

Application:

Reread the verse, substituting your name each time you read the word 'love.' If this is not an accurate reflection of who you are, ask God to help you to become it. This is not easy, your entire default mode will have to change, so be patient but committed to the task.

And remember to look past the superficial—the words and the actions of your spouse, and redirect your gaze instead to their intentions which are often pure and sincere. They just somehow get lost in translation.

Winter Day 6: Snowstorm

Be on your guard; stand firm in the faith; be courageous; be strong.

1 Corinthians 16:13 (NIV)

Going In Blind

A snowstorm prominently features an abundance of two components: snow and wind. It is a very dangerous type of storm as visibility and acoustics are impaired.

There are many heart-wrenching scenes in books and movies where the hero faces the brutalities of a snowstorm to rescue a loved one who is lost in the elements. Without the ability to see or hear properly, their love for the missing person drives them from the comfort and shelter of a home.

There are many metaphoric snowstorms in a marriage. These can include:

- the potential for divorce
- a spouse who is losing their faith
- illness
- a financial crisis
- an affair

Just like in the scenes meant to entertain and touch us, it is our love that drives us to act. Our action, however, is more of an inward process as it involves faith.

A friend once described faith as the force that activates God; whereas fear, on the other hand, activates the enemy. We cannot allow the enemy to gain a foothold in our lives by entertaining fear.

Faith is the only way forward.

Prayer:

It says in Your Word, in Luke 15:7, that the disciples asked for more faith. We also want to come to You, Lord God, and ask for a double portion of faith so that we can stand amidst a storm without wavering. May my faith activate Your power to work in my situation.

Reflection:

God honors faith. What are ways that you can try to increase or solidify your faith?

Application:

Start building your faith on a daily basis:

- Study the Word
- Be in constant fellowship with the Lord through prayer
- Regularly meet up with mature believers
- Listen to the testimony of others
- Worship

- Remind yourself of how God has proven His goodness to you

Winter Day 7: Open Windows

"Forget the former things; do not dwell on the past. See, I am doing a new thing! Now it springs up; do you not perceive it?"

Isaiah 43:19 (NIV)

Try New Things

Whenever a room gets stuffy and stifling because staying warm is a prerogative, nothing brings relief like opening a window and letting a breeze of fresh air in.

There is a boring kind of safety that is brought by locking yourself in a familiar room. You know what to expect, you know what needs to be done, no surprises. This leads to a stale, mundane life.

Have you ever wondered why the Dead Sea in Israel is a *dead sea*? There is no outlet.

We see that change was encouraged in the Old Testament, specifically in 2 Kings 18 where we read about King Hezekiah. This is a man who wanted to please God, like his ancestor David, so

> "[Hezekiah] removed the high places [of pagan worship], broke down the images (memorial stones) and cut down the Asherim. He also crushed to pieces the bronze serpent that Moses had made, for until those days the Israelites had burned incense to it; and it was called

Nehushtan [a bronze sculpture]" (2 Kings 18:4, AMP).

Hezekiah smashed the bronze serpent pole that God told Moses to make during the time when the Israelites were being bitten by snakes in the desert. The pole's time was up. It was no longer effectively serving God's purposes—the people were worshiping the instrument and not the Healer. It had to go.

When Jesus healed the blind in the New Testament, he didn't use the same method.

Because God is always and never the same, it forces us to stay connected to Him.

Prayer:

Jesus, help me to recognize when I am on auto-pilot in my marriage and when I take things for granted. Help me to connect with my spouse in new ways so that we will continue to grow together.

Reflection:

Y0u do not want your marriage to become the Dead Sea, where there is little life. Grow together, don't die together. How are you facilitating growth in your marriage?

Application:

Create a bucket list with your spouse. Try to tick off as many of these items as possible.

Winter Day 8: Snow Day

But Jesus said, "Let the children alone, and do not hinder them from coming to Me; for the kingdom of heaven belongs to such as these."

Matthew 19:14 (NASB)

Becoming Like Children

Most children love a white winter. They get to play in the snow, make snowmen, and have snowball fights. Another white winter perk that kids adore is a snow day: those days when it is impossible to safely get to school.

A marriage is a heart home for two adults. And while it sounds idyllic, it runs the risk of becoming boring and stale. Love runs the risk of becoming passive.

Every day of marriage should be approached with at least the attempt of child-like enthusiasm and passion of a snow day or a snowball fight. These two feelings need to be cultivated, they don't just happen spontaneously after a few years of commitment.

Prayer:

Lord, may we never become a passive member of our marriage. Help us to find innovative ideas to make our marriage fun. May we show the world how incredible a godly marriage can be.

Reflection:

"A successful marriage requires falling in love many times, always with the same person." –Mignon McLaughlin.

Has your love become passive? What can you do to incorporate more passion and pleasure into your relationship?

Application:

Remember what you did at the start of your relationship to make your spouse feel special and your dates memorable. Try to do similar things at least once a week. Start by trying to recreate one of your most memorable dates as soon as possible.

Winter Day 9: Heirloom Roses

"But I lavish unfailing love for a thousand generations on those who love Me and obey My commands."

Exodus 20:6 (NLT)

The Legacy You are Leaving Behind for Your Children

Heirloom roses are considered to be "antique roses" as they have been around for much longer than their hybridized modern counterparts. Heirlooms are also known as the category of roses with a better fragrance and a better chance to withstand the cold as they are hardier than their modern counterparts.

Legacy is a topic that most parents obsess with once children are added to the mix. Some people battle with the concept long before they procreate as the idea of leaving something lasting, meaningful, and significant behind is a powerful, even all-consuming driving force that dictates their behavior.

Have you ever stepped back and considered what are you (a) instilling in those around you with your habits and philosophies, and (b) leaving behind once you no longer find yourself in your earthly shell?

Prayer:

God, thank You for the ability to influence others. Help me to take it seriously as the legacy I want to create for those around me, should be life-giving and kingdom-building. Help me to look further than just the physical. Help me to consider the spiritual inheritance I am building up for generations to come.

Reflection:

Everything you do impacts those around you. Some actions have a larger reach than you can imagine, so be mindful of your behavior. How are you currently impacting your relationship with your spouse?

Application:

Stop every now and again, and ask yourself how that which you are currently doing, will impact those around you. Also consider what your behavior means to the legacy you want to leave behind.

Winter Day 10: Avocados

Be watchful, stand firm in the faith, act like men, be strong. Let all that you do be done in love.

I Corinthians 16:13-14 (ESV)

The Man and Husband

> "When the Aztecs discovered the avocado in 500 BC, they named it āhuacatl, which translates to 'testicle.' It is likely that the texture, shape, and size of the fruit, as well as the way it grows in pairs, inspired the name of the avocado," (Zajac, 2018).

Another possible reason why an avocado is considered a man's fruit is because of its tough skin and big, solid pip. A man is generally known for their toughness and the suppression of their emotions. However, once we get past the gruff exterior, we are met with soft, tender, and sweet flesh.

Because avocado trees originate from Mexico, they like the heat. Just like any hot-blooded male. While it is not impossible for an avocado tree to withstand the cold, it does need a little help. And this is why God created Eve.

Many moons ago, I heard a sermon where aspects of womanhood were likened to the weapons a Roman soldier would fight with. The shield was representative of her prayers for her husband, and the sword was the cause she represented: fighting for those entrusted in her care.

In his book, the 2011 best-seller, *Wild at Heart*, John Eldredge states that every man has three intrinsic desires:

- a battle to fight, since God created him to be a warrior

- an adventure to live, since it is a test put to a man to make him stronger and smarter

- a beauty to rescue, because the Lord made him desire to be the hero to the woman he loves

Prayer:

Husband - Father God, you created me to rule. Help me to rule with love, fight with honor, and learn with grace. Thank you for my precious wife. May I mimic the character of Jesus during all interactions with her.

Wife - Lord God, thank You for my husband. Thank You for the amazing way You have put him together. Give me the wisdom I need to be the perfect helpmate for him.

Reflection:

"What is man, that thou art mindful of him? and the son of man, that thou visitest him? For thou hast made him a little lower than the angels, and hast crowned him with glory and honor. Thou madest him to have dominion over the works of thy hands; thou hast put all things under his feet," (Psalm 8:4-6, KJV).

Do you still consider your partner as profoundly impressive—like you did when you first met? What has happened since then, if anything, that has caused you to look with less than favorable eyes on your partner?

Application:

Pray as a couple and ask the Lord to show you what adventure He has in store for you as a couple, and the respective roles you play in the adventure. Study the Word and other resources if it will help gain a healthy understanding of what a husband's role is in his marriage and in his home.

Winter Day 11: Snowdrops

Then keep your tongue from speaking evil and your lips from telling lies!

Psalm 34:13 (NLT)

Purity of Speech

Snowdrops are often associated with purity because of their white petals.

In a marital context, purity has to do with abstaining from inappropriate sexual acts, yes, but it also has to do with keeping your mind, heart, and mouth free from that which is considered unsuitable.

For today's reading, I want to focus on purity of speech and all that it entails.

Let's start with some questions:

- When you speak of your spouse to others, do you carefully weigh what you say?
- When you speak to your spouse, do you use loving words and a kind voice?
- Can respect, love, and tolerance be found in the tone of your voice when there is a verbal exchange?

After a few years of being married, we tend to lose our sensitivity when it comes to speaking about each other or even defending one another. This especially happens when there have been multiple unresolved issues that have constantly beaten us down. Out of a need for survival, we've turned inward, placing the focus on ourselves.

It is heartbreaking to hear how spouses sometimes speak to one another when the Bible is clear about how we should address one another: "Let your conversation be gracious and attractive so that you will have the right response for everyone," (Colossians 4:6, NLT).

Prayer:

Lord God, I come to you with Psalm 141:3 and ask that You would please put a guard in front of my mouth. Help me to choose my words carefully so that I honor both You and my spouse in my speech.

Reflection:

Be careful little mouth what you say.

Think of the last few times you spoke of your partner. Were they positive statements?

Application:

Practice mindful self-control when it comes to speaking to your spouse. Remember that they are not the enemy and that they deserve your best. They should blossom under your words and not be reduced to feel small, insignificant, or worthless.

Winter Day 12: Winter Olympics

Do nothing out of rivalry or conceit...

Philippians 2:3-4 (NIV)

Competition Between Spouses

Healthy competition exists between competitors. This is something that drives you forward and challenges you to do your best. A marriage benefits from this type of challenge since there is no real comparison happening. It's more like friendly banter while we try to show off a little bit.

Galatians 6:4 (NIV) says, "Pay careful attention to your own work, for then you will get the satisfaction of a job well done, and you won't need to compare yourself to anyone else."

On the other hand, there is rivalry. This is a much less pleasant form of competition. This competition is all about exerting dominance and superiority and can leave the loser devastated.

Luke 16:15 (NIV) says, "And he said to them, 'You are those who justify yourselves before men, but God knows your hearts. For what is exalted among men is an abomination in the sight of God.'"

It is a sad state of affairs when all we care about is being the best. It places the focus on us and causes dissension.

Prayer:

Lord, may we always encourage each other to do our best. May we enjoy healthy competition as it spurs us on to be excellent in all we do. May we never become rivals, set at opposite sides. We are a team and we plan to stay that way.

Reflection:

"Because she competes with no one, no one can compete with her," –Lao Tze.

This is applicable to husbands too: "Because he competes with no one, no one can compete with him." However, does unhealthy competition feature in your marriage?

Application:

Create a space for your spouse and yourself where optimal growth is encouraged because you want to be all that God created you to be.

Winter Day 13: Ice Walking

Search me, O God, and know my heart! Try me and know my thoughts! And see if there be any grievous way in me, and lead me in the way everlasting!

Psalm 139:23-24 (ESV)

Transparency

Have you ever walked on ice where you have been able to look through the ice at the fish and turtles below? It is a magical experience. However, it is also a dangerous place to be. The ice could break.

Transparency in a marriage means that nothing is hidden from each other. There is no need to hide anything because there is unconditional love and acceptance. We share our feelings, thoughts and actions because it is safe to do so. There is also respect so no unnecessary detail is divulged that could hurt our spouse.

Something else that can damage a relationship is when a buried secret is revealed. This shatters trust and causes the spouse who found out about the omission to question everything about the relationship.

Proverbs 28:13 (ESV) says, "Whoever conceals his transgressions will not prosper, but he who confesses and forsakes them will obtain mercy."

It takes a lot of strength and courage to admit something unpleasant to our spouse, but alongside the admission comes the release of a hold that gripped us for far too long. The person trying to come clean should be respected for their brave choice. Something that should also be taken into consideration is that the person who is on the receiving end of the news, should be given time to process the information and not expected to immediately carry on like nothing happened.

Prayer:

Lord, give me the courage to be completely transparent with my spouse. I want them to know me inside and out.

Reflection:

"Reflection and transparency make you vulnerable. Be honest and transparent anyway," —Mother Teresa.

"Transparency is the antidote to hypocrisy," —Britt Merrick.

Is there something holding you back from confessing something to your spouse?

Application:

Make it a policy in your marriage to always be truthful. Start today by committing to be truthful, in a kind and loving way, to your partner.

Winter Day 14: The End of Winter

"Blessed are the peacemakers, for they will be called children of God."

Matthew 5:9 (NIV)

Be a Peacemaker

It is said that once you see a daffodil in bloom you can know that the winter is finally over. This imagery led me to think about another cold and desolate place a married couple may find themselves in—a fight; as well as the metaphoric daffodil who ends the war.

The Word is very clear when it comes to the peacemakers. They are (a) blessed; and (b) called children of God. There is both a reward and an identity attached to the behavior. The identity aspect reinforces that God sees us as His children when we mimic His behavior.

It is hard to be the first one to reach out after a fight. Our pride, and sometimes our wounds, gets in the way.

Sometimes we may reach out to the other person not because we want to, but because we know it is what God expects of us. We choose to honor God by choosing to approach our spouse seeking reconciliation.

The Amplified says in Ephesians 4:26 "BE ANGRY [at sin—at immorality, at injustice, at ungodly behavior],

YET DO NOT SIN; do not let your anger [cause you shame, nor allow it to] last until the sun goes down."

Prayer:

Lord God, help me to be an ambassador for Your kingdom by promoting and actively pursuing peace in my marriage. Help me to recognize the beauty in my spouse, as well as their true intentions, when things have gotten ugly. Help me to be plugged into the Vine so that peace will be a fruit that I bear.

Reflection:

The Lord blesses those who are willing to make peacekeeping a priority. Are you willing to make it a priority in your marriage?

Application:

The next time there is a fight, take a few minutes to process what happened leading up to the argument. During that time also calm your emotions as it is very difficult to have a meaningful talk with someone when there are emotions impairing your judgment. Once you feel calm enough, and your spouse is ready for it, initiate a conversation. It is always a good idea to start the conversation with a prayer.

Conclusion

I said most of what I felt I needed to say in the Introduction, found at the beginning of the book. Therefore, this section will be much shorter than that one. I hope that you, your spouse, and your marriage have benefited from this book.

As mentioned throughout, marriage is sacred to the Lord—it's fundamental to a healthy society. A break-up in the family unit is, in essence, a crack in life's infrastructure. Marriage is also the closest representation we have of the love and unity of the Trinity.

Research done by the Pew Research Center shows, statistically speaking, that less people are getting married today than in past years.. The preferred narrative is called "uncomplicated cohabitation". The message this sends out to the world is in direct contrast to what the Word teaches us.

It is up to us to show the world what they are missing out on if they choose to act outside the will of God.

Finally, I want to leave you with the song that inspires me. It is the song that I walked down the aisle to.

Seasons by Donald Lawrence and The Tri-City Singers (2003)

Oh yeah

I feel seasons everywhere

And I feel blessings in the air

Those seeds that you've sown

It's time to come into your own

Seasons, walk into your season

I know that you've invested a lot

The return has been slow

You throw up your hands

And say 'I give up, I just can't take it anymore"

But I hear the Spirit saying

That it's your time

The wait is over

It's your time

The wait is over

I heard the Spirit say

It's your time

The wait is over

Walk into your season

Hmmmm

Let's walk on everybody

References

Amplified Holy Bible. (2015). Zondervan.

Beaulieu, D. (2021, May 21). *10 Popular heirloom roses for your garden*. The Spruce. https://www.thespruce.com/popular-heirloom-roses-5114930

Ben. (2019, May 24). *Do you need to worry about bears in winter? - Pack your tent*. Pack Your Tent. https://packyourtent.com/do-you-need-to-worry-about-bears-in-winter/

Berean Study Bible. (2020). Whitaker House.

Bissoy, J. (n.d.). *The Fresh Prince of Bel-Air*. Carleton Admissions. https://www.carleton.edu/admissions/stories/the-fresh-prince-of-bel-air/#:~:text=Episode%20Analysis

Bluebell. (n.d.). Woodland Trust. https://www.woodlandtrust.org.uk/trees-woods-

and-wildlife/plants/wild-
flowers/bluebell/#:~:text=In%20the%20language
%20of%20flowers

Dasgupta, S. (2016, May 12). *How many plant species are
there in the world? Scientists now have an answer.*
Mongabay   Environmental   News.
https://news.mongabay.com/2016/05/many-
plants-world-scientists-may-now-answer

Ducharme, J. (2018, June 5). *How to tell if you're in a toxic
relationship — and what to do about it.* Time; Time.
https://time.com/5274206/toxic-relationship-signs-
help/

Eight consequences of being impatient. (2019, March 24).
Exploring   Your   Mind.
https://exploringyourmind.com/eight-
consequences-being-impatient/

Eldredge, J. (2011). *Wild at heart - discovering the secret of a
man's soul.* Thomas Nelson Publishers.

Flower Meanings: The Language of Flowers. (2022, February
2).   Old   Farmer's   Almanac.

https://www.almanac.com/flower-meanings-language-flowers

Forbes, M. (2022, February 25). *Allium flower: Meaning, symbolism, and colors | Pansy Maiden*. Www.pansymaiden.com. https://www.pansymaiden.com/flowers/meaning/allium/

Fry, R., and Parker, K. (2021, October 5). *Rising share of U.S. adults are living without a spouse or partner*. Pew Research Center's Social & Demographic Trends Project. https://www.pewresearch.org/social-trends/2021/10/05/rising-share-of-u-s-adults-are-living-without-a-spouse-or-spouse/

Glass, L. (1997). *Toxic people : 10 ways of dealing with people who make your life miserable*. St. Martin's Griffin.

Got Questions Ministries. (2022, January 4). *What does it mean that God makes our feet like the feet of a deer (Habakkuk 3:19)?* GotQuestions.org. https://www.gotquestions.org/feet-like-a-deer.html

Granny Smith. (2020, June 24). Wikipedia. https://en.wikipedia.org/wiki/Granny_Smith

Harley, W. F. (2020). *HIS NEEDS, HER NEEDS : building a marriage that lasts.* Revell.

Holy Bible : Easy-to-Read Version. (2007). Authentic Pub.

Holy Bible : King James Version. (2016). Christian Art Publishers.

Holy Bible : New Living Translation. (1996). Tyndale House Publishers.

Holy Bible : New King James version. (2016). Struik Christian Media.

Hutchinson, A. (2021, May 19). *Why Do Climbers Really Die on Everest?* Outside Online. https://www.outsideonline.com/health/training-performance/why-do-climbers-die-on-everest/

K, J. (2010, March 25). Spring cleaning is based on practices from generations ago. *The Washington Post.* https://www.washingtonpost.com/wp-dyn/content/article/2010/03/23/AR2010032303492.html

Kilmann Diagnostics. (2019, June 3). *An overview of the Thomas-Kilmann conflict mode instrument (TKI) A long-*

term collaboration by Kenneth W. Thomas and Ralph H. Kilmann - Kilmann Diagnostics. Kilmann Diagnostics. https://kilmanndiagnostics.com/overview-thomas-kilmann-conflict-mode-instrument-tki/

Lewis, C. S., and L'engle-Franklin, M. (2001). *A grief observed.* Harper San Francisco.

Lockman. (1997). *New American Standard Bible.* Foundation Publications.

Mandriota, M. (2021, October 17). *What Is Lust?* Verywell   Mind. https://www.verywellmind.com/what-is-lust-5189688

Marchiano, B. (2000). *In the footsteps of Jesus.* Christian Art Publishers.

Merrill, M. (2017, August 24). *How to achieve unity in your marriage | Thursday thrive from friendship Baptist Church.* Owassoisms.com. http://www.owassoisms.com/achieve-unity-marriage/

Monkshood | AACC.org. (n.d.). Www.aacc.org; Therapeutic Drug Management and Toxicology.

https://www.aacc.org/science-and-research/toxin-library/monkshood

New Living Translation: Life Application Study Bible. (2005). Tyndale.

Noble, C. (2012, September 11). *Fleeing when in conflict.* Cinergy. https://cinergycoaching.com/2012/09/fleeing-when-in-conflict/

ONE | The Potter's House. (2020, March 2). **Marriage | "What You Were Never Told" - Touré Roberts.** Www.youtube.com. https://youtu.be/_9mQfsXPhII

Philipson, A. (2014, July 10). *Eating an apple a day improves women's sex lives, study shows.* Www.telegraph.co.uk. https://www.telegraph.co.uk/women/womens-health/10960228/Eating-an-apple-a-day-improves-womens-sex-lives-study-shows.html

Piper, J. (2016, February 26). *Six things submission is not.* Desiring God.

https://www.desiringgod.org/articles/six-things-submission-is-not

Rellinger, D. (2012, September 17). *Pomegranate: Autumn's nutritional superfood*. MSU Extension. https://www.canr.msu.edu/news/pomegranate_aut umns_nutritional_super_food#:~:text=Pomegranat e%2C%20a%20popular%20fruit%20that

Schreiber, H. (2017, February 6). *Curious chemistry guides hydrangea colors*. American Scientist. https://www.americanscientist.org/article/curious-chemistry-guides-hydrangea-colors#:~:text=Red%20or%20pink%20blooms%20 result

Slager, T. (2018, June 26). *How to have a godly marriage - Ephesians 5:22-33*. Www.youtube.com. https://youtu.be/o8rD-8fz-Fs

Szekely, G. (2017, December 5). *5 Less-known reasons why date night is important*. The Couples Center. https://www.thecouplescenter.org/5-less-known-reasons-date-night-important/

The Crown of Creation | Wild at Heart. (2020, July 20). Wildatheart.org. https://wildatheart.org/daily-reading/crown-creation

The Holy Bible : ESV : English Standard Version containing the old and new testaments. (2008). Crossway Bibles.

The Passion Translation. (2020). Broadstreet Publishing Group, LLC.

Wikipedia Contributors. (2019, April 16). *Wear sunscreen.* Wikipedia; Wikimedia Foundation. https://en.wikipedia.org/wiki/Wear_Sunscreen

Zajac, S. (2018, June 14). *"Avocado" actually comes from a word meaning "testicle."* Business Insider. https://www.businessinsider.com/avocado-history-word-testicle-2018-6?IR=T

Zimmerman, J. (2015, December 1). *Sukkot, the feast of booths (known to some as the Feast of Tabernacles) | Jewish Voice.* Www.jewishvoice.org. https://www.jewishvoice.org/read/blog/sukkot-feast-booths-known-some-feast-tabernacles

Zondervan. (2014). Holy Bible New Testament The Bible for Everyone: New International Version. Zondervan.